TWAYNE'S WORLD AUTHORS SERIES

A Survey of the World's Literature

Sylvia E. Bowman, Indiana University

GENERAL EDITOR

ITALY

Carlo Golino, University of Massachusetts at Boston

EDITOR

Francesco Guicciardini

TWAS 389

Francesco Guicciardini

Portrait by Giuliano Bugiardini (oil on wood)

FRANCESCO GUICCIARDINI

By PETER E. BONDANELLA
Indiana University

TWAYNE PUBLISHERS
A DIVISION OF G. K. HALL & CO., BOSTON

Library of Congress Cataloging in Publication Data

Bondanella, Peter E   1943-
    Francesco Guicciardini.
        B   T '76   160p.   pub. 8"
    (Twayne's world authors series)
    Bibliography: p. 153-57.
    Includes index.
    1. Guicciardini, Francesco, 1483-1540.   2. Italy —
Historiography.
DG738.14.G9B66   945'.06'0924 [B]   75-41388
ISBN 0-8057-6231-0

For D.M.B., F.P.B.,
J.C.B., and G.B.

Contents

About the Author

Peter E. Bondanella received an A. B. in French and Political Science from Davidson College (1966), an M. A. in Political Science from Stanford University (1967), and a Ph. D. in Comparative Literature from the University of Oregon (1970). A specialist in Italian and Comparative Literature, Professor Bondanella is the author of numerous articles on Italo Svevo, Ronsard, Spenser, Machiavelli, Dante, and the medieval lyric as well as *Machiavelli and the Art of Renaissance History* (Detroit: Wayne State Univ. Press, 1973). At present, he is completing a translation of selections from Giovanni Boccaccio's *Decameron* (a forthcoming Norton Critical Edition), a translation of various works by Niccolò Machiavelli (for a Viking Portable Machiavelli), and is working upon a critical study of Italian neo-realism (Twayne) as well as a reference dictionary of Italian literature (The Greenwood Press). Dr. Bondanella has been a Younger Humanist Fellow for the National Endowment for the Humanities (1972-73). After two years at Wayne State University (1970-72), he is presently an Associate Professor of French and Italian at Indiana University, where he teaches courses in Italian, comparative literature, and film.

Preface

Unlike his more famous friend and contemporary, Niccolò Machiavelli, Francesco Guicciardini attained the heights of political power and influence during his lifetime, and his accomplishments are an integral part of the history of sixteenth-century Italy. Because he is less well - known to most English readers than Machiavelli, a brief chapter on his life and times has been included here. Space prohibits a more detailed examination of this topic, but excellent biographical materials are available in English for the reader who seeks a fuller account of Guicciardini's life. The major goal of this study will be an analysis of the writings of Guicciardini.

I have tried to set all of his works in their proper historical context and to relate the important political or philosophical ideas in them to their special style and literary structure. It is my hope that this book will provide the reader with a detailed account of Guicciardini's major contributions to Renaissance thought and will be of use not only to the general reader but also to Renaissance specialists who undertake the task of examining the works of this fascinating individual.

Guicciardini wrote nothing which a contemporary writer might label "literature," for his most important works are historical, political, and philosophical. There are no novels, no short stories or *novelle*, and no poetry here. But a Renaissance reader did not hold our sharp, modern distinction between imaginative literature and factual history or political theory. Prose skillfully written was prized as much in history or social thought as it was in literature, and Guicciardini's historical prose at its best equals or surpasses that of every Italian writer of the sixteenth century except Machiavelli's. Machiavelli, of course, was more versatile, for he not only created a brilliant prose style in his political treatises but also wrote poetry, an excellent short story, and several plays, one of which is easily the best Italian comedy of the period. Guicciardini had none of these talents; yet in addition to his historical or philosophical treatises, he was a master of the maxim, a literary genre most often associated with French writers of the seventeenth century.

Any critical work on Francesco Guicciardini will be heavily indebted to a small group of dedicated scholars who have spent their lives discovering, editing, interpreting, and publishing the various manuscripts, most of which are found in the Guicciardini family archives in Florence. A book of this kind would not be possible without their efforts, and I hope that I have indicated my debt to them in the proper measure. Excellent English translations of the major books are available, but in treating the minor works, I have been forced to supply my own translations. In such cases, I have tried to achieve accuracy and clarity of meaning without, I hope, completely destroying the particular flavor of Guicciardini's prose style.

A National Endowment for the Humanities Younger Humanist Fellowship allowed me to spend an extended period in Florence, where Count Francesco Guicciardini generously allowed me unrestricted access to the family archives and library which has inspired and enriched these pages. An Indiana University Summer Faculty Fellowship enabled me to work freely and to complete the manuscript. Finally, my wife Julia tried her patience with my often prolix prose style in order to make the finished product more acceptable. For all of this support, both financial and moral, I am very grateful.

PETER· E. BONDANELLA

Bloomington, Indiana

Chronology

seilles to arrange the marriage of Catherine de' Medici to the future Henry II of France.

1534   First drafts of *The History of Italy*. Death of patron, Pope Clement VII. Becomes advisor to Duke Alessandro de' Medici until his assassination in 1537.

1537   Instrumental in selecting Cosimo de' Medici to succeed Alessandro. Political eclipse and retirement from active role in Florentine affairs. Revisions of *The History of Italy* until Guicciardini's death.

1540   Death in Florence and burial in Santa Felicità.

CHAPTER 1

Guicciardini's Life and Times

U NLIKE his more famous contemporary, Niccolò Machiavelli, Francesco Guicciardini was born into one of the oldest and most important families of the Florentine aristocracy. In spite of his many undeniable talents, much of his future political success was determined by this simple fact of birth. The origins of the family are somewhat obscure, but by the thirteenth century, its name appears frequently in city records. The Guicciardini held an extraordinarily large number of offices in the government, including sixteen terms as Gonfaloniere of Justice, and forty-four terms as Priors in the Signoria.[1] Such a record places the clan on the level of the Ridolfi, the Strozzi, the Salviati, and just below the Medici in influence and ambition, if not in wealth. The key to the success of Francesco's branch of the family was its continued association with the Medici. Piero Guicciardini (1378 - 1441), Francesco's great-grandfather, was instrumental in bringing about the return of Cosimo de' Medici from exile in 1434. As early as 1416, he had been granted the title of Count Palatine by Emperor Sigismund, but he never used the title in republican Florence out of respect for its popular traditions. Two of his three sons, Jacopo (1422 - 1490) and Luigi (1407 - 1487), continued the family's close ties with the Medici, dedicating a major portion of their time and energies to public duties. As Jacopo's only son, Francesco's father Piero (1445 - 1513) inherited his entire estate and much of the esteem he had gained in Medici circles.

Piero Guicciardini must have been a singular individual. He had more than the usual acquaintance with the humanist learning of his day, knew some Greek as well as Latin, and was a good friend of the philosopher Marsilio Ficino who witnessed the baptism of his son Francesco. Less frivolous than many of his Medici associates, Piero was deeply moved by the evangelistic message of Girolamo Savonarola and his proclamations of the need for spiritual and

ethical reform both in Florence and in the Catholic Church as a
whole. This sincere piety would later cause him to advise his son
against pursuing a career in the church when the death of an uncle
who had purchased his post as bishop of Cortona from the rapacious
Borgia pope, Alexander VI, unexpectedly opened this career to his
son Francesco. In the *Ricordanze*, the short diary from which much
of our information about Guicciardini's life is obtained, Francesco
explains his father's motives:

Piero determined not to have any of his sons a priest, although there were
five of them, because he thought the affairs of the Church were decadent.
He preferred to lose great present profits and the chance of making one of
his sons a great man, rather than have it on his conscience that he had made
one of his sons a priest out of greed for wealth or a great position.[2]

Far more ambitious than his retiring father, Francesco had
this vacant position less as a source of revenue (although he constantly fretted over his salaries in all his posts) than as a means of
becoming a great man in the Church, perhaps even becoming a cardinal. Honor, reputation, power, and the esteem of his patrician
peers were Guicciardini's constant preoccupations throughout his
lifetime. This driving ambition made him the target of considerable
criticism, both among his contemporaries and among his later
scholarly critics. However, Guicciardini's quest for power and glory
was based upon an aristocratic concept of service to one's city and
family which in its best sense, when pursued selflessly, contributed
much to the greatness of the Florentine Republic and the flourishing
of the cultural renaissance in that city. As Guicciardini himself put it
in the *Memorie di famiglia*, another short work describing the accomplishments of his ancestors, he desired but two things: the continued political and economic ascendency of republican Florence
and the glory of his own family.[3] It was to his credit that he always
viewed the successes of his family and of his own career as directly
related to the fortunes of the republic and not as ends in themselves.

I *Youth and Education*

Seeking a vocation which might gain his father's enthusiastic approval and which might also train him for the kind of employment
toward which he was spurred by his ambition, Guicciardini began
the study of law at the age of fifteen. In 1498 he enrolled at the university in Florence; he transferred to the university of Ferrara in

1501 because his father wished to have a member of the family in a more secure city, so that their wealth could be preserved in the event of any political upheaval in Florence.[4] Moving again to Padua he continued his studies from 1502 until 1505, taking his doctorate in November of that year in civil law only, since he felt that the degree in canon law was not worth the extra expense of twelve and a half ducats.[5] The money spent on Guicciardini's education by his father was faithfully recorded and totaled by his frugal, bourgeois son, who, in the *Ricordanze*, frequently intertwines often banal references to financial affairs with matters of great import. It must be understood, of course, that to a Florentine, money was a very serious business indeed.

Guicciardini's subsequent marriage in 1508 to Maria, fourth daughter of Alamanno Salviati, was a calculated political decision which repaid the bridegroom a hundredfold. The Salviati, especially Alamanno and Jacopo his cousin, belonged to one of the most powerful patrician families in the city, and both were strong opponents of the republic which had ruled the city since the expulsion of the Medici in 1494. Like Guicciardini, the Salviati considered the new gonfaloniere, Piero Soderini, a traitor to his class for allowing upstarts such as Niccolò Machiavelli to exert as much influence in the affairs of Florence as members of more aristocratic families. The marriage thus represented an open declaration of Guicciardini's political sentiments, and although his father Piero worried over the implications of such an action, the practical Francesco would not be persuaded: "Nevertheless I determined to take her, because at that time Alamanno and Iacopo were far greater in family connexions, wealth, reputation, and popularity than any other private citizens in Florence. I set great store by such things and therefore wanted their alliance at all costs."[6] Between the spring of 1508 and that of 1509, Guicciardini also composed but left unfinished, untitled, and unpublished, his first major work, now known as *The History of Florence*. It is an accurate reflection of his patrician views, an interpretation of Florentine history from 1378 until 1509 which emphasizes the contributions of the aristocracy to Florentine greatness and criticizes the erosion of traditional Florentine "liberty" brought about by Medici hegemony.

The alliance through marriage with an illustrious patrician house, the reputation of his family, and his own talents brought him rapid success. The entries in Guicciardini's *Ricordanze* soon after 1508 are full of references to various posts, honors, and legal clients that the young man acquired at least partially through the good offices of his Salviati in-laws. Typical of this kind of assistance was the election of Guicciardini as one of the twelve captains of the hospital of the Ceppo. His father-in-law nominated him for this position, and although it was a minor post, the young man's remarks in his *Ricordanze* reflect his evident pleasure and pride upon his admittance into a group including some of the city's best citizens. Also indicative of Guicciardini's thin skin are his careful recordings in this instance, and in several other elections, of not only those men who cast black beans or votes in his favor, but also the names of those (if any) who cast the negative white bean. We can almost imagine him impatiently asking his father-in-law after the end of such a meeting for details on these matters. Lest we overemphasize the importance of Guicciardini's family ties and underestimate his own talents, it must be noted that Guicciardini's father-in-law died on 24 March 1509, and that he could not have assisted Guicciardini any further even had he lived longer. Commenting on the death of Alamanno Salviati, Guicciardini nonetheless expresses respect for the older man's accomplishments and regret that his death cut short further benefits for himself: "It grieved me beyond measure, so that in all my life I had felt nothing to compare with it, having lost so great a father-in-law of whom I had been going to make so much capital."[7]

II *Political Activity*

More important honors from the state were to follow. In late 1511, although yet still legally under the age required to hold such a post, Guicciardini was named ambassador to the court of King Ferdinand of Spain. He left Florence in the beginning of the following year, receiving a handsome *per diem* salary and a large honorarium of 300 ducats, and completed a leisurely journey of almost two months to Burgos, sparing himself no comfort during his travels. During his stay in Spain, Guicciardini began his collection of maxims and sententious observations which would later develop into the *Ricordi*. He also found the time to compose a more important theoretical treatise, known today as the *Discourse of Logrogno*, which is a declaration of the aristocratic principles of government that he proposed for Florence.

Even a cursory examination of the diplomatic correspondence that Machiavelli sent home to Florence during his own missions abroad will suffice to impress upon us the contrast between these two exceptional men who were in the service of the Florentine

Republic at the same time. Machiavelli, the enthusiastic *popolano* (commoner) eager to defend the reputation of his city abroad, is continually humiliated because of his puny salary; he must often entrust letters to Florentine merchants to save postage, and not a few times he is forced to pay his expenses from his own pocket. Once named by his mentor Soderini to head a mission to Germany for which he was certainly well qualified, he is forced to give way to another because of the opposition of the *ottimati* (patricians), the same class that did so much to aid Guicciardini's career. Yet Machiavelli's complaints are less for himself than for the discredit such treatment brought to the reputation of Florence abroad. Guicciardini, on the other hand, is perfectly at ease in his far more important post, although he may have actually done little to deserve the honor, save having been born into a noble family, and he never questions his right to his position. To those who have much, much is given: Guicciardini not only drew a large salary, in contrast to Machiavelli's pittance, but he also received a gift of 500 gold ducats from the king before his return to Florence in 1513. Certainly, such marked contrast partially explains why even Roberto Ridolfi, the foremost biographer of both men, remarks that he has never managed to like Guicciardini, although his intellect is perhaps the one which he respects more.[8] It is hard to resist the temptation to speculate upon what role Machiavelli might have played in the history of Florence had he, like Guicciardini, been born into a more influential family.

While Guicciardini carried out his mission in Spain, the structure of the Florentine political system was undergoing another of its intermittent changes. The republic for which Machiavelli had worked so enthusiastically had fallen, his superior and patron Piero Soderini (the *bête noire* of Alamanno Salviati, Guicciardini, and the *ottimati*) had left Florence, and Machiavelli himself was eventually removed from the chancellery, tortured, and exiled to political oblivion where he began the political writings for which his name is remembered today. The Medici were again firmly in control of the city. Il Magnifico Lorenzo's son Giovanni (now Pope Leo X) was using the resources of the papacy to consolidate his family's counterrevolution. With his nephew Lorenzo (later Duke of Urbino) as the newly proclaimed Captain General of the Republic, and Cardinal Giulio de' Medici (the son of Giuliano de' Medici, il Magnifico's brother) as Papal Legate, there seemed little chance that republican forces could reassert themselves. In fact, only great upheavals in foreign af-

fairs in 1527 again gave the republicans another opportunity to
come to power. Although the Medici hesitated to bestow upon
Lorenzo any title which might be an open admission of their inten-
tions to make Florence their hereditary, familial possession, it was
obvious to all informed observers that their ambitions were far
greater than Lorenzo's post of Captain General suggested. A
government which ignored the rights and privileges of the other
members of the aristocracy must have made Guicciardini uneasy, especially since it was this aspect of Medici rule which he had
criticized in both his *History of Florence* and the *Discourse of
Logrogno*. He nevertheless attempted to gain the favor of the
Medici, hoping to profit from their increased power, much as his
ancestors had before him.

His efforts were highly successful. In 1516, Pope Leo X named
Guicciardini Governor of Modena, recently taken by Pope Julius II
from the Este family. In 1517, the task of ruling Reggio, another
former Este possession seized by Julius, was entrusted to Guicciardini's care. Although these cities were technically properties of the
church, Leo undoubtedly intended to devise some method of adding
them to Medici control of Florence and Tuscany. Guicciardini's
duties as governor were by no means easy ones. Both cities were split
by feuds between the patrician families; each faction had influential
friends at the papal court and usually attempted to have their causes
decided by exerting their influence in Rome instead of entrusting
their cases to the impartial but extremely severe justice of the new
governor. Guicciardini always avoided, whenever possible, what
Machiavelli would call in his *Discourses* "very damaging middle
roads" or the easy path of compromise. Several heads literally rolled
shortly after Guicciardini's arrival in Modena; to avoid papal intervention and possible amnesty for especially influential law-
breakers, he often had his sentences carried out in such a short time
that no word of pardon could possibly arrive to stay his judgments.

Because the stern measures used by Guicciardini quickly took
their toll, Modena and Reggio became peaceful, exemplary models
for the rest of the papal states to emulate. Leo was pleased with his
success, and in 1521 he appointed him commissioner of the papal armies in a war which eventually brought about the capture by papal
and imperial troops of Parma, Piacenza, and Milan from the French.
It was in the field during this war that Guicciardini began the composition of a work we know today as the *Dialogue on the Government of Florence*, completed several years later. More importantly,

Guicciardini finally met Machiavelli in Modena in 1521. Their family backgrounds or political views must have prevented any earlier acquaintance. In fact, Guicciardini's father-in-law had been the severest critic of Piero Soderini, the man to whom Machiavelli owed his position of influence in the chancellery from 1498 to 1512, and it is likely that Guicciardini had agreed with other aristocratic Florentines in their contemptuous view of Machiavelli as Soderini's lackey. Machiavelli had certainly supervised or written some of the chancellery's instructions to Guicciardini before his mission to Spain, but this was a business matter which did not presuppose any personal contact. In spite of their differences, a strong friendship based upon mutual respect developed between the two men, giving rise to one of the most interesting collections of Renaissance letters. Although many of his contemporaries and future critics found Guicciardini to be a cold, calculating egotist, Machiavelli was strongly attracted to this haughty aristocrat.

Cardinal Giulio de' Medici sent Guiccardini to Parma during 1522 to hold it for the church, in order to have him named governor of the city by Pope Leo X. This plan was interrupted by the pope's death and the subsequent dissolution of the coalition of forces he had organized against the French. Parma was almost without defenses, munitions, or supplies. The French saw in Parma's weakness an opportunity to reverse their defeats and to roll back papal power in northern Italy. In the ensuing battle and siege, however, the French were soundly defeated and were forced to depart in humiliation. Nothing saved Parma from capture but the strong-willed governor who rallied both the terrified citizens and the unpaid, rebellious mercenary troops to an heroic effort. In spite of his services at Parma for the church, the new Flemish pope, Adrian VI, eventually gave all of Guicciardini's duties to other men, an action which rightly enraged the proud patrician. The death of Adrian in 1522 after only eight months as pope was, therefore, as much a source of private joy for Guicciardini as it was a cause of public revelry for the citizens of Rome. The new pope, Cardinal Giulio de' Medici, who took the name Clement VII, proved a devoted patron to Guicciardini.

Once again Guicciardini's fortunes became closely intertwined with those of the Medici family. Clement immediately appointed him President of Romagna, a post that not only increased his power and prestige but also his salary. He thus gained jurisdiction over such cities as Imola, Forli, Faenza, Rimini, Cesena, and Ravenna. Guicciardini was soon to discover that the man who had impressed him as cardinal was somehow transformed into a different person after his elevation to the throne of St. Peter. As another historian of the period put it in his history of Italy, Pope Clement "went to a great deal of trouble to develop from a great and respected Cardinal into a small and little respected Pope."[9] Clement would be forced to suffer the eventual domination of Italy by Emperor Charles V, although he did salvage from this disaster the establishment of an hereditary duchy for his family in Florence which would endure into the eighteenth century. The beginning of the end was the battle of Pavia in 1525, when a besieged imperial army suddenly destroyed the French army surrounding the city, capturing both the French king, François I, and the city of Milan. After the French monarch agreed to harsh terms of peace in order to gain his freedom, the Italian powers began to fear the emperor. In these circumstances, Milan, Venice, Florence, the Pope, and France joined in the League of Cognac in 1526. Guicciardini was, in large measure, responsible for convincing Clement to enter into this ill-fated alliance. He was in turn named Lieutenant General of the army and of the Papal States.

III   Maturity and Literary Output

The ensuing war was possibly Italy's final opportunity to maintain any sort of political independence, but it ended in a terrible disaster. The timidity of the commander of the league's forces, Giovanni Maria della Rovere, the Duke of Urbino, was responsible for the loss of Milan and the surrender of Duke Ferdinando Sforza. A brief truce lulled the pope into believing that Charles V had forgiven him for his part in the league. Largely aided by the vacillation of the Duke of Urbino, an imperial army of German infantrymen moved from Bolzano to Rome with almost no opposition. The pope was virtually helpless. Only a courageous Medici condottiere, Giovanni delle Bande Nere, was willing to risk a battle, and he paid for his bravery with his life. Although the commander of this invasion was killed during the initial assault on Roman defenses (according to Benvenuto Cellini, by his own single but miraculously long musket shot), this did not stop the troops from taking the city, since these soldiers were German protestants, driven both by thirst for booty and the chance to despoil the center of the Roman church. What followed was a sack the like of which had not been seen in Rome since the invasions of the barbarians centuries earlier. Clement had just enough time to escape to the Castel Sant' Angelo. All of Italy was stunned.

Clement's difficulties in Rome weakened Medici control in Florence, and on 16 March 1527, just ten days after the sack of Rome, the family was expelled again from Florence for the second time in three decades. A second republic was proclaimed which was primarily based upon greater participation by the middle classes and those elements of the city formerly influenced by the reformer Girolamo Savonarola. These men were particularly suspicious of patricians like Guicciardini who had been instrumental in the Medici government, and their radicalism in turn helped to alienate and drive away many Florentine aristocrats who might otherwise have been happy to oust the Medici in order to gain more influence themselves.

Guicciardini would have preferred a republic after the manner of that managed by Cosimo de' Medici, an oligarchy wherein the *ottimati* still maintained much influence and prestige. He had no particular love for the absolutism and the establishment of a dynasty that Medici rule now represented, but during the course of the rule of the second republic in Florence (1527 - 1530), he and other aristocrats began to feel that little choice was left for them between a radical, popular government which threatened to exclude them from access to power and to tax them heavily, and a Medici absolutism which, at least, would protect their property and prestige at the price of their traditional privileges.[10] Since, as we shall see later in analyses of Guicciardini's works, the aristocrats' concept of "liberty" or even "republic" was far removed from current definitions, it was much easier for many of them eventually to choose the Medici rule as the lesser of two evils. When Guicciardini was relieved of his duties by the capitulation of Pope Clement to the demands of Charles V, he returned to Florence, offering to do what he could for his beloved city through contacts with Niccolò Capponi, the moderate republican leader. Other members of the new government, however, had different plans for the patricians. Like the Medici before them, they began to levy punitive fines and taxes on rich men considered to be enemies of their regime or friends of the exiled Medici. Guicciardini was struck repeatedly by such measures. Furthermore, he was insulted by an investigation into the role he played in the war and into alleged improper usage of soldiers' pay. None of these charges could possibly have been true, for Guicciardini was incorruptible in spite of certain other personal faults. The investigation understandably hurt his fierce pride, and he found himself among other Florentines who lived to regret such false accusations.

During this troubled period in his life, Guicciardini composed several essentially autobiographical works. The *Consolatoria* discusses the relative merits of religion, philosophy, and reason in the solution of human problems. Perhaps as more of a future defense than as a literary exercise, Guicciardini also prepared a work attributed to an imaginary accuser, the *Oratio Accusatoria*, and a reply in his own defense, the *Oratio Defensoria* (left unfinished). He continued to work on his private book of philosophical maxims, the *Ricordi*. In these works, Guicciardini often foreshadows, more than any other writer of the Italian Renaissance, the introspection of Montaigne. Guicciardini also began a second history of Florence, known to us as *Le Cose Fiorentine* or *Florentine Affairs*, which he never finished and which was discovered only in this century. During the years 1529 - 1530, a period of forced retirement from active political affairs while he lived outside of Florence at Santa Margherita a Montici, his friendship with Machiavelli finally bore intellectual fruit with the composition of another unfinished work, the *Considerations on the 'Discourses' of Machiavelli*. The final version of the *Ricordi* was also completed in 1530.

Retirement from the pope's service was not permanent. The Florentine Republic was beseiged by the armies sent by Pope Clement to reestablish Medici control. Their commander, the Prince of Orange, stayed in Guicciardini's villa, and his armies slowly forced the Florentines into submission after an heroic defense. It was perhaps the finest hour of the city's history as a free republic, one last convulsion of that creative energy which was born in the medieval commune and which provided so much of the dynamic force in Florentine intellectual and cultural affairs. Reduced by plague and lack of food, the city finally surrendered under what appeared to be a generous settlement. Clement, however, had become convinced that reform of a repressive nature was necessary to eradicate forever any vestiges of opposition to his family. He sent Guicciardini to accomplish this task, and the gusto with which the latter so successfully completed it did him very little credit. After having witnessed the destruction of so much of his native city, the decimation of its population, and repeated affronts to his sensitive pride, Guicciardini was in no mood for moderation. Although the terms of the capitulation forbade retribution, Guicciardini himself worked more than anyone else to mete out merciless punishment. Not a few of the most important leaders, among them the gonfaloniere Francesco Carducci, were tortured and executed; many others were proscribed and driven out of the city after having their possessions confiscated. It is an episode in Guicciardini's career which is difficult to reconcile with his usual reputation for fairness, especially after he himself had helped to persuade the pope to agree to mild terms of capitulation. He even admitted in a letter to his brother Luigi that the investigation of republican leaders had revealed that "apart from their perverse obstinacy through which they have destroyed the city, the reports do not reveal any of those frightful crimes which were suspected."[11] It is Guicciardini's part in this repression that partially explains the antipathy of so many Italian critics of the nineteenth century, when Risorgimento republicanism looked upon Machiavelli as a precursor of the new nation and saw in Guicciardini the type of man that had been responsible for Italy's problems since the time she lost her independence.[12]

For his part in this affair, Clement rewarded Guicciardini with the governorship of Bologna. His duties also included filling the office of Vice-Legate there. In 1532, he presided over the meeting of Pope Clement and Charles V in that city. Later in 1533, he accompanied the pope to Marseilles to meet the French king. There the agreement for the marriage of young Catherine de' Medici, the last of the legitimate descendants of Il Magnifico Lorenzo, and the future Henry II was signed. It was a momentous marriage for the family fortunes, because Catherine carried Medici influence in political affairs across the Alps to France and even ruled that nation for a time as regent for her son. During the trip, Guicciardini reverted to his former profession as lawyer; he drew up the marriage contracts, revised them, and then corrected them for the final signatures.

During the next year Clement died. Although his successor Cardinal Farnese (Pope Paul III) would eventually offer Guicciardini a post in the administration of the papal states in 1538, it would be refused. By the year of Clement's death, Guicciardini had been outside of Florence for over 20 years since his mission to Spain. Upon his return home, he once more picked up the second history of the city, *Florentine Affairs*, but again left it unfinished. Between 1534 and 1537, Guicciardini became one of the chief advisors of Alessandro de' Medici, a bastard son of Pope Clement (officially identified as the offspring of Lorenzo de' Medici, Duke of Urbino). Clement meant to use Alessandro as part of his scheme to turn Florence into an hereditary duchy, using the power of the papacy as a fulcrum. Guicciardini served Alessandro primarily in the area of foreign policy; but he was also his personal lawyer in a case brought against him in Naples by some of the disgruntled exiles of the second republic. Alessandro treated Guicciardini with more respect than he had ever known before in Florence. Hence, Alessandro's assassination by Lorenzino de' Medici in 1537 was a great shock.

Although Lorenzino had committed tyrannicide in the finest classical or humanist tradition, he fled the city without proclaiming the death of Alessandro, and his lack of courage following his impulsive crime enabled the Medici forces to maintain control of the city. The specter of another radical republic was uppermost in the minds of all the *ottimati*. Their freedom of choice was limited by the hegemony and consequently the veto power over their affairs exerted by Charles V, but they preferred someone over whom they could exercise as much control as possible. Therefore, a handful of citizens led by Guicciardini decided to invest Cosimo, the son of the Medici condottiere Giovanni delle Bande Nere, with the position in order to avoid the foreign regency that would be imposed upon them if Giulio, the four-year-old son of the slain Alessandro, were allowed to succeed his father. Guicciardini's biographer believes that the choice of Cosimo was motivated primarily by Guicciardini's hope that he might be able to exert some influence over the younger man — even though he did not believe too strongly in such miracles.[13] If this was the case, events soon proved him to be correct. One of the major provisions in the agreement that legalized Cosimo's rise to power was that he serve simply as head of the Florentine Republic rather than as Duke of Florence. Even this verbal fiction was destroyed by Cosimo, however, who eventually used the power of the emperor to confirm Florence as an hereditary Medici state. In return for this, of course, Cosimo was forced to bargain away much of the traditional liberty the Florentines had always enjoyed in foreign affairs. The city became for all practical purposes a satellite state of the Spanish Empire, in a game which required only their presence but not their active participation. Perhaps the most tragic aspect of Guicciardini's life is that he played a major role, albeit a most reluctant one, in the eventual eclipse of that city - state system of republican government which he so greatly admired. Machiavelli was fortunate not to live long enough to see the ignominious end of everything he held dear.

Left with no more illusions and with no access to political power, since Cosimo ruled by himself and resented what he owed to the haughty patrician who had attempted to limit his power, Guicciardini finally retired from politics. From 1538 until his death in 1540, he worked on his masterpiece, *The History of Italy*, which he wrote, corrected, and revised many times. He was buried without elaborate ceremony in the family church at Santa Felicità without any ornate monument to mark his grave. As Ridolfi aptly puts it, "always true to himself, the great realist merely consented to the disconsolate reality of death."[14]

Many of his contemporaries, especially the exiled republicans, reviled him in their histories or memoirs for his relationship to the Medici tyrants and his undisguised desire for power and prestige. When his aristocratic views were compared by Risorgimento critics to Machiavelli's more acceptable and popular republicanism (not to mention the contrast of Machiavelli's warmer personality and Guicciardini's patrician airs), it was inevitable that Guicciardini's true stature would remain obscured by prejudice. More important, however, is the fact that only his *History of Italy* and a partial edition of the *Ricordi* were known to anyone before the nineteenth century. Nothing Guicciardini wrote was published during his lifetime, nor was much of this vast amount of manuscript material even intended for publication. It is possible that only *The History of Italy* was deemed worthy by its author for the eyes of other readers, since that work alone was shown to a friend for corrections or suggestions. The titles we now use for his works are primarily the creation of their modern editors, not of the author himself. Giuseppe Canestrini published most of Guicciardini's works between 1857 and 1867, and for the first time in over three centuries, scholars discovered *The History of Florence, Considerations on the 'Discourses' of Machiavelli*, and *Dialogue on the Government of Florence*, in addition to numerous minor dialogues, discourses, private letters, and notes. Only in our own century did Roberto Ridolfi discover and publish what most scholars consider to be the last possible major work left undiscovered, a history of Florence now known as *Florentine Affairs*. The nature and importance of Guicciardini's contributions to political thought and history still represent, therefore, a critical problem for students of the Italian Renaissance.

CHAPTER 2

Guicciardini's History of Florence

CANESTRINI'S edition of almost all of Guicciardini's unpublished and unedited manuscripts revealed for the first time to nineteenth-century Renaissance historians that Guicciardini had composed a history of his native Florence relatively early in his career. This incomplete manuscript contained neither a title nor chapter divisions, and the title by which we know it today, *The History of Florence (Storie fiorentine)*, was proposed by modern editors.[1] The work was composed between 1508 and 1510, a crucial period in Guicciardini's career, since his marriage to a member of the Salviati family in 1508 represented an open declaration of his aristocratic, antirepublican views. It is not surprising, therefore, that this work contains not only a discussion of Florentine history but also an explicit analysis and critique of political regimes that did not correspond to his patrician ideals. There is another aspect of this history, however, which is more personal. If we recall the statement Guicciardini once made about his two driving desires, the glory of his city and the prestige of his family, we find that this double goal lies at the heart of *The History of Florence*. It was precisely at this same time that Guicciardini began his autobiographical *Ricordanze* and his shorter collection of biographical remarks on members of his family, the *Memorie di famiglia*. In his history of Florence, Guicciardini's interest in his family's role in the life of the city is more marked than in the later historical works. The first sentence of the manuscript, for instance, begins with a reference to the 1378 Ciompi revolt "while Luigi Guicciardini was Gonfaloniere of Justice,"[2] but omits the more important historical fact that Salvestro de' Medici was taking advantage of the occasion to insure his family's more illustrious fortunes because of his part in the events following that revolt.

This work gives an account of Florence's domestic and foreign affairs from 1378 (the Ciompi revolt) until the siege of Pisa in 1509; here, the narrative breaks off in the middle of a sentence. There are often lacunae of dates or names about which the author was uncertain and which he would have eventually filled in, had he ever wished to complete the work. Although *The History of Florence* covers a period of 131 years, there is a marked emphasis upon certain phases of the city's development. The main part of the book concentrates upon the period between 1454 and 1509; the period from 1378-1454 is analyzed only summarily. Guicciardini consciously limits his treatment of the earlier years, explaining in the narrative that he stressed the post-1454 era "since no one has written any history that covers the period extending from the Peace of Lodi to the present."[3] But even within this shorter span of time, it is the rise of Lorenzo il Magnifico to power (1470), the expulsion of the Medici, Savonarola, and the new republic founded in 1494 that most interest him.

I *Early Historical Method*

An examination of the historical sources used by Guicciardini in the composition of this work underlines the limitations of his historical method at this stage in his intellectual development. In the rise of modern historiography from medieval chronicle or humanist didacticism, Guicciardini is often cited as the first historian to approach his subject with a respect for documents and an awareness of diverse, often conflicting, source materials. This judgment, however, is based upon the approach utilized in his historical masterpiece, *The History of Italy*. Nicolai Rubinstein has demonstrated that Guicciardini rarely used official documents in this earlier history of Florence; instead he relied primarily upon the Guicciardini family archives containing not only a private library but, more importantly, many official and semiofficial memoranda, letters and reports. This material dealt with events directly related to the family's history, particularly those which had occurred during the tenure of a family member in a position of authority or influence in the city's government.[4] Events related in Guicciardini's *Memorie di famiglia* are often repeated in *The History of Florence*, but frequently Guicciardini omits parts of the narrative in the history or distorts his description of them in the *Memorie*. Guicciardini may also have had access to the *ricordanze* of other families, especially the Salviati, since the custom of writing such personal family diaries was very common in Renaissance Florence. Two additional *ricor-*

danze by members of the Guicciardini family were available to him in the archives as well. Like the Guicciardini, other aristocrats often retained semiofficial reports, memoranda, or diplomatic correspondence for their own purposes, and it was not uncommon for these to be passed around among a circle of friends and colleagues. Finally, Guicciardini seems to have been influenced in his description of Lorenzo il Magnifico by the portrait of the tyrant given by Girolamo Savonarola in his *Treatise on the Organization of Florence (Trattato del reggimento di Firenze)*.[5] More important in his work than the family archives, of course, was the intercourse Guicciardini had with many of the historical protagonists in those events which occurred during his own lifetime. It is this closeness to his sources that explains in large measure why Guicciardini's history still retains a freshness and a spontaneity which do not fail to intrigue the modern reader, however slight his knowledge of the intricacies of Florentine politics may be.

With his history of Florence, Guicciardini consciously followed a classical tradition established by the early Florentine humanists. The composition of histories of Italian city - states had a long and venerable tradition in the Renaissance.[6] The humanists of the fifteenth century set the tone of historical narrative in Italy by elevating the classical example of Livy's account of republican Rome into a model of what eloquent, learned historical narrative should be. Leonardo Bruni and Poggio Bracciolini, both chancellors of the republic during this period, wrote Latin histories of Florence; Machiavelli's *History of Florence (Istorie fiorentine)*, composed after Guicciardini's *History of Florence*, represented a continuation of this civic history composed by members of the Florentine government. In praising Livy in particular, and the historiography of Greece or Rome in general, the humanists had reacted against the chronicles of their medieval predecessors Villani and Compagni who cared little for logical organization, eloquence of style, or the search for cause and effect. It was not uncommon to find in such medieval histories matters of the greatest historical import mixed with affairs of the most trivial nature in no apparent order whatsoever save a loose fidelity to chronology. The humanists saw in the classics not only a stylistic model but also a sense of purpose and of meaning in history which medieval chronicles lacked, and their sense of civic pride demanded that they elevate Florence to rival Athens or Rome.

The humanists regarded history as a branch of rhetoric, an instrument by which men could be taught ethics and proper social conduct, and their most common stylistic tool was the *exemplum*. It was the concrete example or illustration of a moral precept that was most effective; as they put it, history teaches by example (*per exempla docet*). Since history was a didactic genre, the kinds of archival research and the meticulous verification of source materials we insist upon today as the most basic aspect of the historian's task were less important in the Renaissance. The historian was more apt to follow a single source than he was to examine all available reports in order to construct his own analysis of any situation or event. As Felix Gilbert describes this historiography, "not factual completeness and accuracy, but moral guidance was expected from the true historian, and he was therefore permitted to select and to stylize the events of the past."[7] Still, this did not elevate blatant falsification to the status of historical truth; the boundaries between historical truth and literary fiction were simply less rigid than we believe them to be with our present distinctions between history and literature.

What is most striking about Guicciardini's first history of Florence, however, is its relative independence from the classical or Renaissance Latin models. While it is true that Guicciardini adopts the view that history teaches by example, he nevertheless avoids the almost obligatory presentation of stereotyped battle scenes, paired sets of highly rhetorical speeches representing conflicting points of view held by historical figures, or the general introductions with philosophical reflections common to both classical and humanist historiography. What attracts his attention, and what is still alive in the work after over four centuries, is his treatment of character, his sketches of several important individuals. The presence of these character sketches enables the writer to assess events as a product of the traits of their protagonists. Guicciardini usually presents his portraits after the death of his subject in an *elogium*, an assessment of the man's achievements which he combines with an examination of the relationship between the character's personality and his deeds.[8] Such a technique was not peculiar to classical or humanist historiography, however, and it can also be found in medieval chronicles, although these chronicles show less concern with psychological motivations and greater interest in the moral ramifications of men's deeds. *The History of Florence* was therefore undertaken without the grandiose literary pretensions other such histories embraced. Roberto Ridolfi claims that it has "the natural style, the simplicity and the energy common to all Florentine authors of that time who were content to write as they spoke; with this difference, that the good homespun of Guicciardini's prose is always further supported by the thread of a vigorous line of thought."[9]

While his history is motivated by his general political views, Guicciardini only rarely comments on the theoretical foundations of his works, and it is therefore somewhat difficult to reconstruct his ideas about the nature and function of history except by analyzing his own attempts in this genre. One remark, however, in his *Ricordi* (number 143) reveals that he was very dissatisfied with all historians in one respect:

they failed to set down many things which were known in their times, supposing them to be too well known. . . . But if they had considered that in the course of time cities decay and the memory of things is lost, and that histories are written for no other reason than to preserve that memory in perpetuity, they would have been more diligent in writing them down. Thus all these things could be as clear to one born in a distant age as to those who were actually present, which is the real purpose of history.[10]

The desire to preserve even minor details is most evident in *The History of Florence*. Guicciardini goes to great pains to list members of diplomatic missions, members of various committees, results of elections, and the like. Such details make the work an important, though not always accurate, source for contemporary studies of Renaissance Florence. Nevertheless, the most instructive aspect of this passage from the *Ricordi* is what Guicciardini omits, the complete absence of the traditional humanistic definition of history as a tool to teach and instruct in order to improve men's conduct. Admittedly, the final version of the *Ricordi* is a product of a much later and more pessimistic period in Guicciardini's life, but the constant reference to history as a practical guide in the earlier works of the humanists of the Quattrocento as well as in the works of Machiavelli written after the composition of Guicciardini's *History of Florence* underlines the fact that history, in Guicciardini's opinion, had a more humble role. He believed its real purpose to be that of preserving the memory of the past. This definition was no doubt nurtured by Guicciardini's aristocratic background with its concern for family and tradition. But Guicciardini's notion of the profoundly elegiac function of history also reflects a pessimism which negates history as a positive, morally redemptive force for the reformation of the present or the future.

Machiavelli's enthusiastic citations from the classical historians were intended to incite his contemporaries to emulate ancient *virtù* in order to bring about a political and military renaissance that would complement the literary and artistic revival in Italy. Guicciardini's sadder and limited, but perhaps wiser, view of history as a memorial to a past which quickly fades away reveals a more tragic conception of man and his possibilities, almost a Vergilian compassion for the *lacrimae rerum*, the tears in the nature of things. The chasm separating the two Florentines in this regard illustrates not just a difference in personality but also a growing shift in perspective as the optimism of the early Renaissance faded into tragic resignation caused, at least in part, by Italy's gradual political eclipse. Guicciardini did not despair of history's power to teach men about the past. His doubts, later expressed in a more systematic fashion in both his *Ricordi* and his *Considerations on the 'Discourses' of Niccolò Machiavelli*, were directed not so much towards the problem of learning from the past as to the practical application of such lessons for the present or future. While *The History of Florence* might not contain a set of rules for political conduct, it could at least assist the reader in the rational analysis and the intellectual comprehension of the errors committed by men of another epoch. Such an exercise of reason, the supreme human faculty, was in and of itself a praiseworthy thing for Guicciardini.

II *The Golden Age*

This view of the past implies, of course, an interpretation of the political systems Florence had experienced during the period under study. Guicciardini is quite naturally a partisan of an aristocratic oligarchy, rule by the *ottimati* or the best citizens of the city. In one sense, therefore, the work represents a critique of both Medici tyranny and republican demagoguery with its accompanying anarchy. Machiavelli's golden age was the Rome of Livy, the era of republican self-sacrifice and discipline which he hoped, through an act of will and of faith, could be superimposed upon the corrupt city of Florence. If Guicciardini ever envisioned a golden age for Florence, it was not the age of Lorenzo il Magnifico (as we might think today) nor any past epoch from classical antiquity; it was, instead, the period from 1393 to 1420 — long before Cosimo de' Medici had begun to alter the oligarchy which ruled Florence behind the screen of republican institutions. Guicciardini's definition of the excellence of this period is one based upon his class prejudices:

Florence was successful both at home and abroad; at home, because it remained free, united, and governed by well-to-do, good, and capable men; abroad, because it defended itself against powerful enemies and greatly expanded its dominion. Florentine successes were so great that this government is deservedly said to be the wisest, the most glorious, and the happiest that our city had had for a long time.[11]

This idyllic situation was to change rapidly with the gradual concentration of power in the hands of one man, Cosimo de' Medici, and his descendants. Piero Guicciardini (Francesco's great-grandfather) had been instrumental in the return of Cosimo from exile in 1439 and in the eventual destruction of the patrician oligarchy. Guicciardini never criticizes the part his own family played in this development; like so many aristocratic intellectuals of this or other periods of history, he preferred an oligarchy but ultimately chose to accept the destruction of political liberties in order to safeguard the rights of property and the access to prestige upon which the political power of the aristocracy was originally based. Consequently, although he consistently criticizes both Medici tyranny and republican excess, he will consistently, both in his actions and in his works, lean toward the system which best guarantees the privileges of his own particular class.

This aristocratic point of view gives the work its theoretical focus. Characters and events described in the history are judged in terms of this predominant ideology. Cosimo is criticized for exiling many of his noble opponents after 1439 and for replacing them with "many vile men of low station" over whom he had complete control. Guicciardini recounts that when "someone warned Cosimo that getting rid of so many noble men was unwise, he is said to have replied that a few lengths of expensive cloth would fill Florence with aristocrats — implying that honors and riches make vile men noble."[12] This indignant comment reflects Guicciardini's point of view concisely. In Guicciardini's opinion Lorenzo was more to blame than his grandfather Cosimo. Not only did he prohibit marriages between patrician families which might strengthen opposition to his power, but he also appointed plebeians to posts of authority. As Guicciardini lists some of Lorenzo's appointments, the tone of the narrative becomes bitter and sarcastic: "a man like Antonio di Bernardo, though only a craftsman, was raised to prominence by being put in charge of the Monte"; "And ser Giovanni, the legislative notary, was the son of a notary from Protovecchio"; "Messer Bartolomeo Scala, son of a miller from Colle, rose from the position of senior chancellor of the Signoria to become Gonfaloniere of Justice, much to the outrage and contempt of all the leading citizens."[13] Guicciardini never says that these men were not competent individuals; his basic complaint is that they were not of gentle birth and that they depended upon Lorenzo's favor more than upon their own resources or ancestry.

In Guicciardini's opinion, the aristocrats fared no better under the republic formed after the expulsion of the Medici. They had been instrumental in changing the government, since they had hoped to return to the kind of system that had prevailed before 1439. Within the institutions of the republic, they wanted to reestablish what was usually called a *governo stretto* ("narrow" or restricted government). Their opponents, largely from the middle class, wished to maintain and even to increase the *governo largo* ("wide" or less restricted government) instituted in 1494 and encouraged by Savonarola and his followers. Florentine political strife had, therefore, begun to develop into overt class conflict.[14] Hoping to use the need for a permanent executive as an excuse for asserting their own power, the aristocrats, led by Alamanno Salviati, supported Piero Soderini for election as Gonfaloniere for life. His subsequent refusal to cooperate with their plans led to increasing resentment among the patricians, especially among the Salviati. Guicciardini, like his father-in-law, considered Soderini a traitor to his class and rarely admitted in his history his many excellent qualities as an administrator:

His conduct in office aimed at gaining the favor of the people and pleasing the multitude. Instead of calling meetings of the leading citizens to consult on important matters of state, as his predecessors had done continually since '94, he called meetings only very seldom, preferring instead to consult the Colleges, whose members were almost always and almost all little men of little quality.[15]

His descriptions of Soderini's followers are always critical. They are variously described as "worthless and ignorant men," "poor and ignorant," men of "little capacity," while the aristocrats are consistently "men of quality," "noble men," "men of experience." Such a deep-seated hatred of Soderini by a whole class of Florentines explains why Machiavelli, his trusted confidant in the government, met with such opposition when Soderini wished to send him as ambassador to Germany. As Guicciardini reports the incident, "many well-to-do men demanded that someone else be sent," since there were "many young men of quality well equipped to go, they said, and it would be a good way to give them some experience."[16]

III   The Balance of Power: 1494

Besides this central ideological aspect of Guicciardini's *History of Florence*, another major concept shapes the presentation of the narrative. This is Guicciardini's interpretation of 1494 as a turning point in Florentine and, to a lesser degree, Italian history.[17] Before the invasion of Italy in that year by Charles VIII, King of France, the Italian citizens of the various city - states, principalities, and kingdoms had generally believed that Italy did exist as an objective intellectual and cultural entity in spite of the many political divisions within the peninsula. Most Italians considered the territory beyond the Alps to be inhabited by "barbarians," nations culturally inferior to any of the several important Italian states, each of which had a distinct but nevertheless recognizably Italian culture. Most cultivated foreigners during the Renaissance considered Italy to be the model for civilized behavior, the arts, and learning that would be followed for almost two centuries, and their evaluation, although perhaps a bit exaggerated, was not too far from the truth. The distinction between the "barbarian" and the "cultured" had classical antecedents in a similar feeling held by the Greek city-states confronted by Rome, and subsequently by the Romans themselves. In all three cases, however, the apparent artistic, cultural, and intellectual superiority held by Greece, Rome, and Florence was insufficient to save any of them from eventual decline and eclipse as a result of the military and political superiority of their opponents. Written in 1508 - 1510, Guicciardini's *History of Florence* could not encompass the ultimate results of this gradual development in Italy which had the most serious consequences for Florence. Although he saw clearly the beginning of the end for Italian independence, in this early history, the event is viewed primarily from a Florentine, and, therefore, a relatively parochial point of view. This would be replaced in *The History of Italy* by a less Florentine and more broadly European assessment of the tragedy of Italy, defined in more clearly national or cultural terms.

Guicciardini's description of the beginning of this momentous historical event is drawn with a precision and a sense of drama that seem to belie the fact that this was the work of a novice in the field of historiography:

A fire and pestilence had entered Italy. States toppled and the methods of governing them changed. The art of war changed too. Before, nearly all of Italy had been divided among five states: the Papacy, Naples, Venice, Milan, and Florence. Each tried to preserve its possessions; each was concerned that no one should occupy anyone else's territory or grow strong enough for the others to fear. . . . When war did break out, the sides were so evenly balanced, the methods of warfare so slow, and the artillery so inefficient that it took nearly a whole summer to take a castle. Wars were very long, and battles ended with few or no deaths. The French invasion, like a sudden storm, turned everything topsy-turvy. The unity of Italy was broken and shattered, and gone were the care and consideration that each state used to give to common affairs. . . . Battles were fierce and bloody. And finally, states were maintained, ruined, given, and taken away not by plans drawn up in a study, as used to be the case, but in the field, by force of arms.[18]

The concept of the balance of power is implicit in this analysis of how Italians managed their internal affairs until outsiders destroyed the equilibrium. Lorenzo de' Medici, in Guicciardini's view, was instrumental in making this system of checks and balances possible, and while he was in control of the city, Florence "had become virtually the fulcrum of all Italy."[19] The calamity that overtook Italy was, however, seen by Guicciardini as a human phenomenon, an historical fact which was comprehensible through the use of human reason. The events he describes are attributed to human errors and psychological traits (greed, ambition, fear, and hatred) and not to some divine punishment of Italy for its "sins" — as preached by reformers like Savonarola. For Guicciardini, what could be known about human history might be limited, but it could only be discovered through a rational study of human nature combined with a philosophical consideration of the power of chance or *fortuna*, a concept that became more and more important in the historiography of the period. Fortune, however, was far removed from the type of transcendental explanations proposed by medieval historians; it did not represent the intervention of divine purpose or providence but, instead, encompassed all that was contingent and unpredictable in human behavior, all that escaped the realm of predictability or rational explanation. Any rationality inherent in human affairs, limited as it might be, was generally revealed by a study of the personal attributes of the movers of these events. Guicciardini's interest in psychological motives and explanations for the behavior of his historical protagonists is, therefore, an integral aspect of his historical narrative. And this conceptual preoccupation produces a stylistic counterpart in his work, the character sketch.

IV   *Historical Character Sketches*

The part of *The History of Florence* which most interests a modern reader, apart from the work's status as an expression of a particular class consciousness or its usefulness as a source of information, is essentially that part devoted to literary portraits of central figures in Florentine history. We shall examine only the most important subjects in the work, Cosimo and Lorenzo de' Medici and Girolamo Savonarola. Guicciardini's distaste for the system developed by both of the Medici, which robbed many aristocrats of the influence and prestige he considered to be their legitimate due, did not cause Guicciardini to underestimate their accomplishments. He remarks that the two were so outstanding that "Italy had no private citizen comparable with them since the fall of Rome."[20] He then devotes a part of his narrative to a comparison of the two men. Such biographical comparisons are not frequent in this work, but this one is particularly felicitous and foreshadows the famous contrast of the two Medici popes, Leo X and Clement VII, in *The History of Italy*. The taste for such comparisons was no doubt acquired through his reading of Plutarch's *Parallel Lives*, a work which became one of the most popular books in sixteenth-century Europe.

Lorenzo de' Medici is pictured by Guicciardini as an infinitely complicated man, a mixture of impressive virtues and several serious vices. His intellect is viewed as sounder than his judgment (although that was usually good), and this led him to foment several impetuous and costly actions, such as the rebellion of Volterra. Guicciardini himself felt that this quality had become disproportionate, for he carried his desire to excel over others even into matters of little importance and was angered if anyone tried to equal or surpass him in trivial games or in composing verse. He is described as a miserable businessman, unlike Cosimo, and he spared no expense to impress important people, even if that meant dipping into public funds to meet his own needs. Guicciardini's description of Lorenzo's physical appearance is a testament to his quest for historical honesty and realism: "Lorenzo was of medium stature, with an ugly, dark face, though of a grave air. His voice and pronunciation were harsh and very unpleasant; he seemed to speak through his nose."[21]

The comparison of Lorenzo and Cosimo shows how subtle Guicciardini's political judgments were even at this early period in his intellectual development. Of the two men, Cosimo is assessed to be the superior. It is important to note that Guicciardini's aristocratic viewpoint does not influence this conclusion. Although Lorenzo did more than anyone before him to destroy the oligarchy dear to Guicciardini — so that during his day Florence was ruled by a tyranny "even though it could not have had a better tyrant or a more pleasant one"[22] — the belief that Cosimo was a greater man is based solely on concrete achievements in the light of the potential of each man. Although less of an intellectual, Cosimo's judgment was sounder; he not only ruled Florence for thirty years without any serious opposition (unlike Lorenzo, whose ambition to dominate sparked the Pazzi plot and resulted in the death of his brother Giuliano), but he was also a consummate businessman. Cosimo left many works and public monuments that made Florence one of the world's most beautiful cities; Lorenzo left few and wasted most of his inheritance on spectacular gifts and shows for foreign monarchs. Cosimo's political skill was superior, for he founded the dynasty. Lorenzo had only to maintain this inherited power, but this he did only with difficulty, provoking foreign adventures and an Italian alliance against Florence which Cosimo would most certainly have avoided. Although Cosimo lacked eloquence and any literary talent, his virtues were substantial ones and his contributions durable.

Guicciardini's judgment has influenced our own opinions of the Medici ever since *The History of Florence* was first published, much as Guicciardini's *History of Italy* has always played a major role as a source of both information and opinion in the interpretation of the contributions and characters of various historical protagonists of the Italian Renaissance. Even though Guicciardini's characterization of these two men is intriguing, there are few surprises. Machiavelli says approximately the same thing in his *History of Florence*, and since Guicciardini's work remained unpublished until the nineteenth century, it was Machiavelli's portrait of these two men, and not Guicciardini's, which was to be more influential in shaping the judgments of future historians. Of greater interest, and directly contradicting everything Machiavelli ever wrote on the subject, is Guicciardini's portrait of Girolamo Savonarola, the remarkable priest

who exerted so much influence upon the fortunes of the Florentine
Republic from the time of the expulsion of the Medici until his execution in 1498. Machiavelli's contemptuous remarks about un-
armed prophets in *The Prince* (chapter 6) pertain directly to
Savonarola. In another letter, Machiavelli cannot avoid referring to
Savonarola's profoundly religious message as "lies."[23] It seems that
Machiavelli was simply incapable of comprehending anything of a
spiritual nature, although his own praise of Rome often betrays the
fervor of a secularized religion. Guicciardini, often viewed as a
cynical, egotistical realist even when compared to Machiavelli, surprises us by his deeper understanding of what Savonarola
represented for the history of his city. He is ambivalent about the
divine origin of Savonarola's mission. He notes, for example, that
the leading citizens accepted the friar's proposal of a government
modeled upon the one in Venice "either by divine inspiration or by
his own art"; elsewhere, he states that "it seemed that everything
Brother Jerome proposed had more than human force."[24] Many of
Florence's leading citizens, both intellectuals and businessmen like
Guicciardini's father, were profoundly touched by the sincerity and
the simplicity of Savonarola's call for reform within the church. It
was the influence of Savonarola that saved Guicciardini from an
ecclesiastical career; he even collected extracts from many of the
friar's sermons.[25] It did not escape Guicciardini's attention that Pope
Alexander VI (the Borgia pope made notorious primarily by Guicciardini's later description of him in *The History of Italy*) led the opposition to Savonarola within the church and was largely responsible
for his execution. Because of the friar's sermons, Pope Alexander ex-
communicated the city of Florence, and the resultant business
losses, perhaps more than anything else, led to a reaction in Florence
against the friar.

Guicciardini described Savonarola's execution as "shameful"; his
only vice, if he had any, was that of ambition, a sin which Guicciardini found especially easy to forgive in any great man. His reformation of Florentine morality was praised without reserve by the
somewhat puritanical Guicciardini: "Nor had there ever been as
much goodness and religion in Florence as there was in his time.
After his death, they disappeared, showing that whatever virtue
there was had been introduced and maintained by him."[26] Guicciardini furthermore insisted that Savonarola alone enabled the republic
to maintain a certain stability after the expulsion of Piero de'
Medici. His concluding *elogium* of the man underlines both his

realistic approach to the priest's virtues and his awareness, in contrast to Machiavelli, of the spiritual power of his appeal:

Because the results of his works were so good, and because several of his prophecies were fulfilled, many people continued to believe for a long time that he was truly sent by God and that he was a true prophet, despite the excommunication, the trial, and his death. For my part I am in doubt, and have no firm opinion on the matter. I shall reserve my judgment for a future time, if I live that long; for time clears up everything. But I do believe this: if he was good, we have seen a great prophet in our time; if he was bad, we have seen a great man. For, apart from his erudition, we must admit that if he was able to fool the public for so many years on so important a matter, without ever being caught in a lie, he must have had great judgment, talent, and power of invention.[27]

Guicciardini's *History of Florence* has been widely used as a sourcebook for Renaissance Florence since its publication over a century ago. One important question connected with this work, therefore, is its value as true history, as factual narrative. Renaissance historians used criteria for the selection of their "facts" which would offend modern historians, and Guicciardini was no exception. For example, in more than a few cases, he omits important information about his own family's part in supporting the Medici, usually because such information would not have found a welcome audience in the Florence of 1510. And yet, in other instances, he gives too much credit to his ancestors and ignores the more important deeds of others. Admittedly unfinished, the work nevertheless contains factual errors as well as lacunae in the manuscript. The nucleus of his great works is already apparent, however, in the penetrating analysis of character, the self-confident judgments of crucial events, and the powerful, dramatic style.

As a source of information to contemporary historians, *The History of Florence* is more useful for the period after 1494, that is, the period when the young historian had the advantage of his personal contacts with many important citizens who had participated in the events about which he wrote. Although the history is marred by a parochialism inherent in its genesis within the tradition of the autobiographical and familial diary, it was this very narrow interest which initiated Guicciardini's interest in historical narrative.[28]

Critical discussion of *The History of Florence* has revolved around the problem of the relationship of history and politics in the work. One important view of the work refuses to see it as anything but a political treatise and defines it as the presentation, within an aristocratic ideology, of Guicciardini's critique of both the republic and the Medici regime.[29] Most recent interpretations of the work, however, have rightly rejected this facile separation of history from political theory. It is precisely the connection of these two interests in Florence that produced a flowering of such works as those of Machiavelli or Guicciardini. In Guicciardini's case, a close acquaintance with practical political affairs in conjunction with a desire to glorify and preserve his family's memory led to a work which integrates both politics and history. Although the work is marred by an undue emphasis upon family affairs — to the disadvantage of other events — it was precisely Guicciardini's desire to produce a synthesis between family and political history that led him to investigate the social behavior of Renaissance man.

CHAPTER 3

The Road from History to Political Analysis

THE integration of historical investigation and political theory in Guicciardini's works was a gradual development, one in which *The History of Florence* plays an important but secondary role. Although this history contains the nucleus of such a synthesis, it is primarily an expression of a class ideology without a methodological rigor and a logic of argumentation to support its assertions. The link between this early historical work and the later, better-known writings is found in the several discourses or dialogues that Guicciardini completed between 1512 and 1525. They include the following titles: *Diary of a Journey to Spain* (1512); *Report on Spain* (1512); *Discourse of Logrogno* (1512); *On the Government of Florence after the Restoration of the Medici* (1512); *On the Method of Securing the State for the Medici Family* (1516); and the *Dialogue on the Government of Florence* (1521 - 1525).[1] None of these works have been translated into English.

Both the *Diary of a Journey to Spain* and *Report on Spain* relate experiences Guicciardini had during his mission as ambassador to the Spanish court just before the fall of the Florentine Republic. The first work is almost wholly devoted to simple remarks that any traveller might make in a travel diary; it is of only slight interest to us here. Whereas the autobiographical impulse that was central to the genesis of *The History of Florence* is also present in the *Diary*, thus denying it any historical or political significance, the *Report on Spain* is much more revealing. It presents a picture of Spain drawn by a member of a self-consciously superior foreign culture. It is historically and culturally important, therefore, and presents a kind of national character sketch of the Spanish people. Machiavelli attempted the same kind of portraiture during his diplomatic missions abroad. Guicciardini's judgments of Spain correspond to many other assessments of that nation made by other Italians after him.[2]

He finds the same national character traits that have, over the years,
become an accepted stereotype: avarice, arrogance, haughty pride,
and an inexhaustible capacity to react impulsively to any slight to
one's honor. Guicciardini also thought that the often praised piety of
the Spanish was simply superficial; few men he met in Spain were as
sincerely religious as the average Florentine merchant. His criticism
of the Spanish nobility because of their aversion to any kind of work
reflects the bourgeois nature of the Florentine aristocracy. He notes
that skilled artisans in Spain are almost always foreigners, and that
the Spanish despise letters of all kinds.

The result is a rather bleak picture painted by a man who ob-
viously felt he was living in a culturally underdeveloped area. What
is most important in this work, however, is Guicciardini's search for
a psychological profile of the entire Spanish nation, his attempt to
delineate rationally those qualities common to all men of that ascendant nation in order to analyze, interpret, and perhaps even predict
their political behavior. In this sense, his personal experiences have
already begun to become part of his theoretical pronouncements on
politics, even though the latter appear here only in an embryonic
stage, without the methodological rigor or systematic presentation
of future works.

Never transcending their narrow subject matter, the two works on
Spain remain more important as autobiographical documents than
as works which figure in the development of Guicciardini's historical
and political ideas. The major event that occurred while Guicciardini was in Spain was the fall of the republic in 1512 and the
restoration of the Medici. Current affairs and political theory were
always closely connected during the Florentine Renaissance, and
this event too inspired many treatises, discourses, and dialogues.[3]
The grave constitutional problems arising from the many sudden
political upheavals that Florence experienced between 1494 and
1530 produced a rich political literature, and consequently, an interest in historical investigation among Florentine intellectuals unparalleled in any other nation of Europe during the Renaissance.
Guicciardini and Machiavelli are only two representatives of a much
larger intellectual current which raised the discussion of human
social behavior to a level of sophistication which far surpassed the
speculative philosophy of the same period. Guicciardini was interested in constitutional problems even before the fall of the
republic made the subject a necessity for any Florentine discussing
his city's government.

I *The* Discourse of Logrogno

Much of the ideology of *The History of Florence* reflects at least an implicit preference for reform in favor of rule by the few capable men of the aristocracy. A key document in his views on Florentine affairs, the *Discourse of Logrogno*, was completed shortly before the government of Soderini collapsed. The *Discourse of Logrogno* presents many of the demands of the Florentine aristocracy of the period. Furthermore, it offers suggestions for constitutional reform from which Guicciardini never essentially deviates in his other works.[4] Instead of abstract, vague ideal schemes, Guicciardini presents concrete proposals for a complete revision of the Florentine constitution. His suggestions, however, are still tied closely to the urgency of the moment and are not yet purely theoretical formulations based upon a systematic political theory. The model state proposed by Guicciardini is essentially based upon his interpretation of the constitution of Venice.[5] He accepts the two constitutional innovations of the Venetian republic, proposing a gonfaloniere, the executive, with lifelong tenure as well as a Grand Council which would consider legislative proposals and elect members of important committees. His main concern, however, is the moderation of both the excessive power of any executive who holds office for life and the corresponding ignorance of the "people" in the Grand Council. To guide the ship of state through this narrow passage between tyranny and anarchy, Guicciardini advocates the creation of a third force, a Senate of about two hundred members who would hold office for life. Eighty would be elected by the Grand Council and thirty by various executive committees; the rest of the men would be former gonfalonieri, past members of important committees, military commissioners and ambassadors. The Senate would control foreign policy by appointing all ambassadors. Members of important boards, although elected by the Grand Council, would be Senators. Most importantly, the Senate would have total control of the purse strings. It would also debate all legislative proposals, thereby limiting the jurisdiction of the Grand Council to only those proposals forwarded to it by the Senate. The three elements in this proposal correspond both to many contemporary interpretations of the republican government in Venice as well as to classical ideals of mixed government. In theory, the gonfaloniere, the Senate and the Grand Council correspond respectively to the monarchical, aristocratic, and democratic elements discussed by both Aristotle

and Polybius as well as many Renaissance humanists, including even
Machiavelli in his *Discourses*.

In discussing such terms as democracy, aristocracy, liberty, and
the like in relation to the Florentine state of Guicciardini's day, it is
absolutely essential not to confuse what was then called a "popular"
or "democratic" government with our own understanding of these
terms. Von Albertini notes, for example, that only 3,200 of some
90,000 citizens were even entitled to representation in the Grand
Council of the republic as a result of the reforms brought about after
the election of Soderini as gonfaloniere in 1502,[6] and Guicciardini
certainly had no intention of increasing access to political power.
This small percentage of eligible voters is far removed from any-
modern concept of universal suffrage. Moreover, not all the citizens
of this group were given the right to become members of the Grand
Council. Only a small and well-defined middle class of artisans and
businessmen actually obtained the right to sit in assembly; workers,
who comprised a large segment of the general populace, were excluded. Hence, the republic was, in our terms, an oligarchy. So
narrow a definition of the "popular" element within the constitution
proposed by Guicciardini perhaps better than anything else helps us
to comprehend just how few citizens he included in the ranks of the
aristocracy. He also expected that the executive would reflect the
aspirations of the nobility, not the "people," itself a limited group.
To Guicciardini even the concept of the "people" meant not the
masses but only those inhabitants of Florence who possessed the
right to participate in the public life of the city or to hold office.[7]
Before we dismiss the discussion of popular government as simply a
means of disguising an oligarchy, let us bear in mind that in its day,
the republican government of Florence was probably the most
democratic government in the world regardless of how far it seems
removed from our modern understanding of that concept. Furthermore, we would do well to remember that the phrase "We, the
people" of our own constitution originally covered neither slaves nor
women, and that very seldom anyone but property owners received
all the benefits of citizenship in the early years of our democracy.

The *Discourse of Logrogno* is thus an explicit and more systematic
expression of the class ideology implicit in *The History of Florence*.
Government is still viewed as an art capable of being mastered by
only a few men, but Guicciardini acknowledges the reforms of the
republic in the inclusion of the executive and of the Grand Council.
When we compare the Senate's duties to that of the Grand Council

and bear in mind the limited access to the Grand Council, it is immediately apparent that the task of the so-called "popular" element of the state would often simply be the affirmation or rejection (but not the initiation) of proposals previously debated in the Senate. Such was Guicciardini's proposal for reform, an ideal not completely impossible to realize before the fall of the republic, a utopia based more upon historical precedent or institutional reform than upon philosophical speculation or flights of the imagination. Several general ideas contained in the *Discourse of Logrogno*, however, transcend the specific limits of this program of reform. Since Guicciardini examines the institutional organization of the republic, he is forced to define the nature of such abstractions as "the state" and "liberty." His definition of the state sounds more like the statement of a modern positivist than the opinion of a Renaissance man: "The state and empire are nothing but violence over subjects, disguised in some cases by some honest title; to wish to conserve it without recourse to arms or one's own forces, but simply with the aid of others, is like trying to practice a trade without the tools proper to that trade."[8] A similar refusal to dress the state in the idealistic terms of either classical or humanist rhetoric reflects the same kind of honest realism we also find in Machiavelli's *Prince*, a work written in the following year. Liberty, far from being a morally redemptive spirit, is simply "nothing more than the predominance of laws and public order over the desires of single individuals."[9] Liberty is therefore "law and order" administered and enforced without regard to a person's social class or personal beliefs; the justice of the laws enforced, however, is not even mentioned.

Although often considered a cynic, Guicciardini differs from Machiavelli in his view of human nature. While Machiavelli felt men were basically evil, he nevertheless built his political theory on the almost impossible task of transcending this defective human nature. Guicciardini, less optimistic about the chances for a rebirth of classical virtue in Renaissance Italy, nevertheless notes in the *Discourse of Logrogno* that the natural inclination of man is to "follow the good," but he qualifies this optimistic statement by noting that man naturally follows the good if his personal self-interest does not divert him from that path.[10] Self-interest and the role of the *particulare*, as Guicciardini puts it, become a crucial element in his thinking. Unlike his later writings, where Guicciardini often criticizes Machiavelli for references to ancient practices, Guicciardini himself makes numerous general references to the past in both the *Discourse of Logrogno* and in the later *Dialogue on the Government of Florence*. There is even a Machiavellian tone in his suggestion near the end of this discourse that the reform of a city is a "divine act."[11]

The most revealing remark in the *Discourse of Logrogno* also contains the only poetic images in the work. Guicciardini rejects half-measures or minor reforms and says that true reform should proceed in a radical manner: "I do not see how one or several limited laws can bear fruit; it would be necessary to put everything in a heap and to reduce all this mass to one form, and then to reshape and to redefine this form in the same way that a baker makes things to eat from dough: if the first shape does not come out well, he makes a heap of everything and gives it a new form; there is also the example of good doctors who find a body full of so many illnesses that they cannot treat it with a single intention, and so they apply themselves to clearing up all the symptoms with medicines and to creating with the entire body a new disposition, an action which, if difficult and requiring a good doctor, is yet not impossible."[12] The analogy of the statesman to the baker implies that institutional reform may bring about the creation of a new form of government or, more importantly to men of Guicciardini's class, may allow the reshaping of a government to bring it back to a former and more desirable condition. It is an optimistic assertion similar to Machiavelli's belief that governments could and should be brought back to first principles. However, the second analogy of the statesman to the physician requires some explanation in spite of its familiar sounding ring. Machiaelli's famous references to the statesman as a physician in *The Prince* are aimed at an entirely different problem. For him, the ruler must be like the doctor in detecting the symptoms of disease in the body politic at an early stage in their development so that drastic cures are not required. His foresight will avoid the illness entirely if possible. Guicciardini seems to feel that Florence has more serious maladies than Machiavelli imagines, for his statesman-physician must content himself with only patching up the patient. His predictive powers in the future go unmentioned. Guicciardini's limited and less ambitious view of the statesman's possibilities is consistent with his habitual refusal to base political behavior upon abstract schemes projected into the future. Nevertheless, Guicciardini's belief that government will yield to human will and that the society in which man lives is a product of his own desires and plans links

Guicciardini not only to his humanist predecessors but also to his contemporary Machiavelli, in spite of all their other differences. It is this faith in man's potentiality to fashion his own political environment that is responsible for much of the vitality and the brilliance of Florentine historical and political literature during the Renaissance.

II *Two Minor Treatises*

After the collapse of the Florentine Republic, Guicciardini became closely connected with the Medici family because of the various positions he held in administering church properties for Leo X. It is not surprising, therefore, that during this time he should write several brief discourses concerning the Medici and their role in Florentine affairs. In the earliest of these two treatises, *On the Government of Florence after the Restoration of the Medici*, Guicciardini argues that moderation in dealing with their rebellious former subjects is the only method to assure the Medici of their power in Florence. While many men have remained implacable opponents of the Medici since 1494, others have only become enemies out of necessity to conform to the will of the majority and can therefore be easily persuaded to support the family again, provided that they receive a fair share of the honors and prestige that the family will be able to control. By concentrating upon this class of men, the Medici can, in Guicciardini's opinion, win the support of a group whose self-interest will lead it to oppose the more recalcitrant opponents of the family.

The second and more interesting treatise, *On the Method of Securing the State for the Medici Family*, contains the argument that moderation is the best policy for the returning Medici. Guicciardini especially urges that the family maintain close ties with the aristocrats and that it not count too heavily upon the aid of Pope Leo X, since such influence will disappear immediately after the pope's death. In this treatise, there is a marked philosophical attitude which goes beyond a simple interest in immediate policy. Guicciardini maintains that the way to win political support is through an appeal to a man's self-interest, his *particulare:*

More than anything else, men are moved by their self-interest which is the ruler of all men. It is this which makes them your friends and partisans; I do not deny that certain natural inclinations of love or hate are not also important. But joined to self-interest, these emotions are stronger and more efficacious and without it, they are cancelled.[13]

Guicciardini's belief in the power of man's selfishness reveals his realism, but he joins this remark with one much more cynical, a statement that a realist such as Machiavelli would have denied: "there is no one in Florence who loves liberty and popular government so much that he would not turn to another government with all his soul if he were given more power and a better position than he feels he has in the free government."[14]

Such a statement reveals how Guicciardini's realism excluded most of the ideals of his day except, of course, the firm belief in the superiority of any government organized around the aristocracy. Neither of these short discourses represents a major text in the body of Guicciardini's writings. They do, however, illustrate a departure from many of the other treatises written during the same period by other Florentines who wished to persuade, advise, or often simply to flatter the Medici during a period when the form of the future state in Florence still seemed to be in question. Unlike many of the theorists of his time, Guicciardini addresses himself not only to the interests of the Medici. Instead, his two treatises are intended to persuade the Medici to follow a course of action which is moderate and which would hopefully unite the interests of the family and those of the city.[15] Although he was always anxious to gain the favor of a powerful patron, Guicciardini never forgot that definition of a true aristocrat's behavior first entered in his youthful diary. Without the glory of the commonwealth, all of the power and prestige he amassed for himself and for his family was meaningless. Like the *Discourse of Logrogno*, both of these works respond to a concrete and therefore limited historical situation. Unlike that treatise, however, they propose no substantial constitutional changes, no institutional reforms. They merely counsel a general point of view which is fundamentally designed to salvage as much influence as possible for the aristocrats under Medici rule. An indication of the deterioration in political possibilities for Guicciardini and those of his class can be measured by the figures of speech Guicciardini employs for the ruler in these two brief works. The baker-statesman capable of restoring the material of the body politic to its original form now disappears and only the more traditional images of the ruler as physician or helmsman are present. As is emphasized in the most recent analysis of these treatises, neither of these images offers much comfort to the reader, for the first implies a possibly fatal illness in the body politic while the second points to the existence of a storm buffeting the ship of state.[16]

III *The* Dialogue on the Government of Florence

The *Dialogue on the Government of Florence* marks a return to a systematic and more philosophical examination of Florentine politics and is by far the most important of the minor discourses and dialogues we shall examine in this chapter. Unlike the *Discourse of Logrogno*, this work (consisting of a preface and two books) is presented as a conversation among four men: Piero Guicciardini (the author's father); Bernardo del Nero (a supporter of the Medici executed by the republic in 1497); Piero Capponi (symbol of aristocratic opposition to Medici rule); and Paolantonio Soderini (follower of Savonarola and a strong proponent of popular government). The form of this work thus follows the extremely fashionable humanist genre of the dialogue-debate, and it has been suggested that Guicciardini selected this form after a reading of Machiavelli's dialogue, *The Art of War*.[17]

The literary pretensions of the work, regardless of the source of the inspiration of its form, are evident in an analysis of the three revisions of the text; almost all the changes the author makes in successive versions are stylistic ones.[18] It is likely, therefore, that Guicciardini did envision the publication of this work at some future date, and this alone sets the dialogue apart from most of his works about which he had no expectation concerning publication.

The content of the second book of the dialogue follows much of what Guicciardini had written earlier in the *Discourse of Logrogno*. The Venetian model for the Florentine constitution is defined as the best possible form of government with its mixed constitution and its safeguards against both popular anarchy and the tyranny of the executive. It is the first book, however, which reveals an original approach significant in the development of Guicciardini's mature political philosophy and his use of historical investigation as an instrument for the study of politics. The argument is developed through a debate between Capponi and Soderini on the one hand and Bernardo del Nero on the other; Guicciardini's father, as in life, maintains a neutral detachment. Guicciardini's own opinions are voiced by Bernardo del Nero. Although he was a strong partisan of the Medici, Bernardo does not reject the critique of their form of government as a tyranny — as asserted by Capponi and Soderini. On the contrary, he admits that both Capponi's and Soderini's views have validity. But his main argument and, therefore, that of Guicciardini, is that the reorganization of the state after 1494, and the expulsion of the Medici, have not only not resolved old problems but have even created new and more serious ones. Bernardo criticizes Capponi for holding firm to the now impossible and utopian aristocratic dream of a return to things as they were before 1439. Soderini's error is his reliance upon highly abstract arguments and his failure to apply the lessons of the historical experience of Florence to his idealistic theories of popular government. Even the neutral Piero Guicciardini may be seen as the contemplative humanist whose classical culture failed to produce effective action in a concrete social situation. This portrait calls attention to the uselessness and impracticability of much humanist learning. Bernardo indirectly rejects one of Guicciardini's major arguments in *The History of Florence*, for he attacks the idea that Florentine government before 1439 was either perfect or free. As he puts it, it too was another oligarchy disguised behind a democratic facade.

It is not the content of this dialogue which is important, since much of what Bernardo (or Guicciardini) advocates here has already been set forth in the *Discourse of Logrogno*. His point of view, the criteria of his arguments, and the methodology used in arriving at approximately identical conclusions, however, represent a turning point in his thinking. The importance of this dialogue lies in its relationship to the *Ricordi;* there is not a single theoretical idea in the work which does not bear the imprint of this greater work, generally considered to be Guicciardini's political masterpiece which he was revising during this period.[19] Thus, many of the ideas with which Guicciardini's name has long been connected are found first in this lesser-known treatise. In spite of frequent references to the classics in the work, Guicciardini stresses the primacy of experience over theory in politics. He notes that all theories have exceptions and that the practical application of any philosophical scheme can only succeed when the politician possesses discretion, a virtue indispensable for any statesman.[20] The cornerstone of Guicciardini's future mature works, and also the nucleus of his critique of Machiavelli, this principle is followed by the corollary that political change in and of itself is not desirable. Political upheavals can only be assessed by their effects in the real world and not by the degree to which they conform to some ideal political scheme.

As Guicciardini bluntly puts it, "the desire to dominate and to have superiority over others is natural in men," while the love of liberty is much less strong; anyone who has the opportunity to rule others, including those who profess themselves to be lovers of freedom, will do so without the slightest hesitation.[21] Consequently, he rejects as irrelevant much of the energy expended in humanist circles over the "best" or most "natural" kind of government suitable to Florence; in his view no state can exist without force. Legitimized violence, as Guicciardini said earlier in the *Discourse of Logrogno*, is the essence of the state. Men, in fact, love justice more than liberty,[22] and a republic's only theoretical justification is that it may offer more justice than other forms. If the type of tyranny practiced by the Medici succeeds in convincing the citizens that they are being treated equally, men will not hesitate to prefer that form of government without freedom over another kind of government which is closer to the republican ideal.

The fine distinctions made by many aristocrats between one form of oligarchy which they termed a republic and another narrower form of oligarchy, the rule of the Medici, which they called a tyranny are thus revealed to be verbal fictions. The results of a political system are for Guicciardini the determining factors in the analysis of any form of government. Because of this new point of view, a new analysis of Lorenzo de' Medici emerges in this work which corrects and modifies that found in the earlier *History of Florence*. While Bernardo admits that Lorenzo was a tyrant, he also notes that Lorenzo's actions followed a rational, logical, and therefore, for Guicciardini, commendable course of action. With his decisions, Lorenzo, in most cases, attempted to reconcile the interests of his own family with those of the city at large.

Guicciardini more clearly defines his views on the nature of man and on the role of the state and its laws in the *Dialogue on the Government of Florence*. Unlike Machiavelli, who believed men were naturally evil but nevertheless capable of achieving social good by the strength of supreme will, Guicciardini unequivocally declares that "by nature all men are inclined toward the good, nor is there any man who by nature does not prefer the good when presented with an equal opportunity of choosing between good and evil; and if any such men could be found, they would be very rare indeed, and would merit rather to be called beasts than men, since they would lack that inclination natural to almost all men."[23] However, Guicciardini adds that "human nature is very fragile, so that for very frivolous reasons it is diverted from the proper path."[24] Human passions, cupidity, and self-interest, the omnipresent *particulare*, keep man from choosing the good he instinctively recognizes and from acting upon it. This idea is essentially that first expressed in the

Discourse of Logrogno, but Guicciardini now goes beyond this first definition of the vulnerability of human nature, manifest in its penchant toward the *particulare*, to give the state and its laws a positive role in correcting human nature. Necessary evils in human society, the state and its institutions should "maintain men firm in their first natural inclination" toward the good; laws and their rewards or punishments are the "spurs and brakes" without which men would never permanently choose the proper activities necessary for the organization of society.[25] The state must act to force man to follow his better nature. This uneasy combination of human innocence and the corrupting influence of human self-interest is remarkably close to ideas found several centuries later in the works of Jean-Jacques Rousseau, especially in the *Discourse on the Origins of Inequality* and in *The Social Contract*.

In the proposal of a mixed government and in certain key ideas on the nature of man and the state, the *Dialogue on the Government of Florence* reaffirms the basic thrust of the *Discourse of Logrogno*. The methodology and consistent point of view based upon recognizably new criteria make it, however, by far the most important work Guicciardini completed before the *Ricordi*, the *Considerations on the 'Discourses' of Machiavelli*, or *The History of Italy*. First of all, a striking depersonalization of political theory characterizes this dialogue.[26] Many works of the period, Machiavelli's *Prince* being the most notable example, dealt with the qualities requisite for the ideal ruler. Such treatises ranged from the scandalous realism of Machiavelli to more traditional portraits of the Christian Prince like that of Erasmus. Believing that social institutions sometimes shape human behavior more than attributes of human personality, Guicciardini avoids a concentration upon personalities and stresses the importance of institutions and institutional reforms. Implicit in his works is the conviction that a state properly ordered can function reasonably well even with men whose abilities are not always outstanding. The limitation of Guicciardini's approach is partially explained by its strengths. In spite of his more careful analysis of Florentine society and its institutions, Guicciardini failed, unlike Machiavelli, to recognize the ultimate and almost inexorable development in Florentine politics from a republican form to a hereditary principality. Guicciardini's views are sound, but they do not see beyond the situation of 1512. Although Machiavelli too would return to his republican dream in his *Discourses, The*

Prince (written in 1513) clearly envisions the kind of ruler that would prevail in Florence after the rise to power of Cosimo I de' Medici and the eventual establishment of a dynasty that lasted until the mideighteenth century. In this instance, Machiavelli's poetic imagination produced a more accurate prediction of future events than Guicciardini's more sober historical analysis and constitutional proposals.

The acceptable point of view in the dialogue is an analytical one based upon the criteria of rationality and efficiency. Abstract schemes and utopian pronouncements on the nature of the "best" or most "natural" form of government in Florence are rejected. Only the effects of any particular state are calculated and evaluated in deeming that state worthy of blame or praise. The *Dialogue on the Government of Florence* may still ultimately reflect a class bias, but it gives this ideology a firm theoretical, logical, and historical basis and thus transcends the simple reflection of a personal opinion presented with little methodological rigor in *The History of Florence*. Felix Gilbert rightly calls this work the "most characteristic example of integrating history in a work of political theory."[27] Guicciardini's ideal state with its mixed constitution was perhaps itself an abstraction, an unattainable utopia, since it ignored the increasingly inevitable move in Florentine affairs toward the establishment of a principality.[28] But only modern hindsight makes it possible for us to judge errors of this type. The more important part of the work is its spirit, its use of history as a means of political analysis. From a detailed study of Florentine political and constitutional history, Guicciardini deduces the outlines of what he considers to be the best possible form of government for his city. Although the passage of time has revealed his ideal to have been an impossible goal, this should not obscure the essential novelty of his method. For the first time in the development of modern social thought, history has become a tool for the analytical study of political behavior.

CHAPTER 4

An Introspective Interlude

F AR reaching changes in the political system of the Italian peninsula occurred between the time Guicciardini began the composition of the *Dialogue on the Government of Florence* (1521), the final revisions of the *Ricordi*, and the beginning of *The History of Italy* (1527 - 1534). As President of Romagna and the intimate advisor of Pope Clement VII, Guicciardini was for a time one of the most important men in Italy, and his close association with the Medici family increased his access to the councils of the pontiff. The ascendant hegemony of Emperor Charles V in Italy was the dominant political fact of the period. After the disastrous defeat of the French army at Ravenna (1525) and the capture of the French monarch, François I (released in 1526 only after signing the humiliating Treaty of Madrid), even the emperor's Italian allies began to fear his power, and this fear helped to generate the nucleus of an alliance against the emperor. Although Pope Clement was initially uncertain about which side to favor, Guicciardini's influence was apparently the deciding factor in his decision to support the League of Cognac. Guicciardini considered membership in this league to be the last opportunity to salvage what was left of the political independence of the Italian city - states.

The plans of the alliance were not, however, destined to succeed. On 6 May 1527, Rome was attacked and sacked by imperial troops. Locking himself within the strongly fortified Castel Sant' Angelo, the pope barely escaped capture, and the League of Cognac dissolved. Shortly thereafter (16 May), the republican forces took advantage of Clement's predicament by restoring the republic in Florence and by expelling the Medici family from the city. His patron defeated, his post rendered meaningless by military defeat and the new regime, Guicciardini returned to Florence for the first time after many years of service outside of Tuscany. As part of the aristocratic class in Florence which had always supported the institution of a *governo stretto* (restricted government), and as a faithful servant of two Medici popes, Guicciardini was suspected by the more radical republicans of harboring sympathy for the exiled Medici. Moreover, he was accused of embezzling monies appropriated for the support of the papal armies in the League of Cognac. He succeeded in proving his innocence, since the accusation was more a pretext to embarrass a friend of the Medici than a serious charge based upon sound evidence, but Guicciardini was afterward excluded from any public office and was forced to retire from public life to his nearby villa at Finocchieto.

A more precipitous fall from prestige and power to ignominy and disgrace could not be imagined. A lesser man than the strong-willed Guicciardini might never have recovered from such a reversal of fortune. The experience produced, however, three autobiographical works which reveal to us more of Guicciardini's personality than anything else he ever wrote. The longest of these, the *Consolatoria*, deals directly with his personal tragedy. The other two, the *Oratio Accusatoria* and the *Oratio Defensoria*, contain, respectively, a formal accusation for crimes Guicciardini allegedly committed while he was Lieutenant General of the papal forces in the League of Cognac, and Guicciardini's response in his own defense. It is unfortunate that none of these three works is available in translation and that most studies of Guicciardini have consistently overlooked their pertinence.[1]

I *The* Consolatoria *and Self-Analysis*

The *Consolatoria* reveals Guicciardini not as the dispassionate, scientific observer of historical and political facts but as an individual struck by severe misfortune who seeks within himself a rational explanation for his personal tragedy and some modicum of consolation in the face of extreme unhappiness. The style and form of the treatise are rhetorical and at times somewhat heavy, but the sincerity of the sentiments expressed in the work cannot be questioned. Roberto Ridolfi, one of the few critics to have appreciated the importance of this work, calls it the "quintessence of Guicciardini's spirit."[2] The method of self-analysis employed here is akin to that found in the political dialogues. It is a self-conscious search for the truth in a particular historical situation coupled with an attempt to generalize the findings to a level of universality. Guicciardini clearly states that his misfortunes lie not in the loss of political power or financial gain (although this loss was very considerable) but in the stains on his personal honor and family reputation. A stoic acceptance of misfortune is impossible for him, since his sense of indignation and wounded pride cannot allow him to accept the false accusations of the radicals in Florence. Moreover, for a man so basically secular and rational in his outlook, the consolations of religion can assist Guicciardini no more than those of speculative philosophy or dialectics. All that is left for him is a solace "more according to the nature of men and of the world."[3]

Since consolation of this sort is based solely upon the comforts of human reason, Guicciardini's attitude resembles that expressed by Montaigne in his *Essais*. Guicciardini's assessment of the faculty of reason and its role in human life is illuminated in a discussion of his own part in the League of Cognac. Although he advised the pope to enter the disastrous league against the emperor, Guicciardini admits that he made an error of judgment in advising this course of action. He denies, however, any personal guilt or wrongdoing, because his views were not motivated by personal ambition or maliciousness but were only an expression of his desire to secure the well-being of the papal states and the political independence of Italy. Reason, even in the hands of a wise man, cannot be considered infallible, but it is the only instrument man has in his daily struggle against the capricious forces of fortune. Wise men must follow the dictates of reason, even if they fail in the attempt; only fools act against the rules of rational conduct. The paradox, keenly felt by Guicciardini, is that wise men often fail after following a rational course of behavior while fools who disregard the dictates of reason sometimes succeed against all logical expectations. Uncertainty is simply part of the human condition. If the dictates of reason were not to be followed, says Guicciardini, "advisors of princes would be placed in an untenable position if they were obliged to bring into their counsels not only human considerations and rational discourse but also the judgments of astrologers, the prognostications of spirits, and the prophecies of friars."[4]

Guicciardini defends the quality of ambition as a most worthy trait in all great men. It was his own ambition which offended his opponents most strongly, and Guicciardini freely admits that it is his most basic personal characteristic. When directed toward the proper goals in either public or private life, however, Guicciardini notes that it is this attribute which makes men most like gods. Fortune does not always permit a man to express his legitimate ambition within a particular social framework, however. In a most uncharacteristic reference to parallels in ancient history, Guicciardini cites other great men falsely accused of crimes to demonstrate that so-called calumnies as his are actually a proof of superior virtue. The most personal remark in the *Consolatoria* is Guicciardini's own admission that the rewards of success are often bittersweet. Power and honor rarely bring the personal satisfaction most men crave when they seek to obtain them.

The *Consolatoria* reveals a psychological dimension of Guicciardini that belies the description of Guicciardini as a cynical analyst devoid of properly human emotion or sentiment. It is an aspect of the writer that is never recorded in his other historical works. As a writer whose basic instrument was the application of reason to problems of importance, the ultimate rejection of sophisticated philosophical rationalizations contained in rigid systems or theological argument founded upon the authority of ecclesiastical dogma is not surprising. Guicciardini admits for himself and for mankind no other weapon against the vagaries of fate than human intellect, but he realizes that even this last best hope is proven fallible, both in his own life and in the lives of the best of men.

II *Legal Arguments as Intellectual Exercises*

Although there is some debate among scholars concerning Guicciardini's motives for composing the *Oratio Accusatoria* and the *Oratio Defensoria*, it seems most likely that both were composed solely as intellectual exercises based upon hypothetical accusations. The first work argues the case for the prosecution, and the second outlines, in an unfinished form, Guicciardini's own defense. Since the crimes discussed in the two debates had already been successfully defended earlier, it is not likely that these works were written to serve a practical purpose. When Guicciardini was finally condemned in absentia and suffered the confiscation of his goods during the siege of Florence in 1529, it was his association with the Medici, and not theft of public funds, that constituted a crime in the eyes of his enemies, the radicals in control of Florence during the siege of 1529 - 1530.[5] Because Guicciardini was a lawyer by profession, the composition of such imaginary arguments would have seemed no more unusual to his contemporaries than the moot courts conducted in our law schools seem to us today.

The *Oratio Accusatoria* alleges that Guicciardini embezzled funds during the war against the emperor (the same problem discussed in the *Consolatoria*). Guicciardini's imaginary prosecutor is one of the

accused's childhood playmates. The accusation is expressed in a
highly rhetorical, Ciceronian style which strikes the modern reader
as artificial but which is probably an accurate reflection of sixteenth-
century legal language. It abounds in *adynata* or "natural im-
possibles" ("If they could speak, the birds, the rocks, the trees would
proclaim your guilt"), hyperbole ("There is no name to fit the
crime, not even Demosthenes nor Cicero could invent one; it is a
crime which has more heads than Hydra"), and personal invective.[6]
Often, the charges are completely ridiculous. Besides the sack of
Rome and the devastation of the Tuscan countryside by soldiers
whose pay was supposedly embezzled by Guicciardini, Guicciardini
is blamed even for low interest rates in a bank and for the invasion of
Hungary by the Turks. This kind of bombastic rhetoric gives the
reader the impression that the verdict of innocence has already been
rendered by the author.[7] The lack of any essentially dramatic element in the work and the absence of any problematic character in
the accusation is certainly a major barrier to an appreciation of the
speech. It is possible that Guicciardini may have also intended the
accusation to present in a satirical manner the point of view of the
radical republicans, the *arrabbiati* ("mad dogs") who gained control
of Florence shortly before the siege by imperial forces began in
1529. Their hatred of the patricians, particularly those aristocrats
who had ties with the Medici, was well known, and the sometimes
ludicrous arguments in the speech of one of their group could well
be Guicciardini's sly method of composing for his eyes only a private
joke, a satire which would in some measure compensate him for the
trouble these men brought upon him.

Although many elements of the accusation are fantasies, Guicciardini's ambition, by his own admission, was his most salient quality.
Thus, the prosecutor notes that when he knew the young boy years
earlier, Guicciardini was called "Alcibiades" by his friends.[8] The
reference to the overreaching troublemaker of classical Athens was,
in the eyes of the prosecutor, ample proof of Guicciardini's innately
evil character. It is also the kind of biographical detail which, seem-
ing factual, Guicciardini might have inserted in the speech to make
the accusation somewhat credible. The picture drawn of Guicciardini as Governor of Romagna is also probably accurate, for he was
not a man to spare expense on luxury or prestige:

It is certain, your honors, if you had seen Mr. Francesco in Romagna (as I
believe many present have) with his house full of tapestries, of silver objects,
of servants, with the run of the whole province (since he had no other

superior besides the pope, who gave him full authority), with a bodyguard of more than a hundred men with halberds, with other mounted guards always circulating through the city (numbering always in the several hundreds), and if you had seen him never ride forth with less than 100 to 150 horsemen, or if you had witnessed him drowning in such titles as "Your Lordship" or "Most Illustrious Lord," you would not have recognized him as your compatriot or equal. Considering the breadth of his authority, his great dominion and government, his court and its pomp, he would have appeared to you more like a duke or a prince.[9]

To present himself in such a manner (even if only for his own amusement) required no small amount of self-awareness on Guicciardini's part. He knew his defects as well as his virtues. The distaste for such pomp and luxury portrayed in the prosecution's description of his life in Romagna is an accurate reflection of the point of view of the merchants and the middle-class artisans or burghers from whose ranks the Florentine republicans sprang. The rejection of the trappings of the nobility in other cities was still characteristic of the Florentine ruling class during the days of Cosimo de' Medici, who advised his sons to avoid at all costs such ostentation in order to minimize popular resentment of their rule and in order to perpetuate the myth that their family was only "first among equals" in the city. Guicciardini never seemed to share this traditional prejudice against such princely customs, and he never acquired the businessman's distaste for luxury or for extravagance.

The *Oratio Defensoria* remains unfinished. In contrast to the bombastic rhetoric and the fantastic charges of the *Oratio Accusatoria*, the style of Guicciardini's defense is completely different. Citing concrete evidence and documenting his assertions, Guicciardini's defense is based upon logic rather than emotion; a clear and simple presentation of his case stands in sharp contrast to the verbal complexities of the prosecution. In spite of the simpler style and the honesty of the sentiments expressed in this speech, the *Oratio Accusatoria* still remains the most interesting of the two works. Guicciardini reveals more of his personality in this imaginary attack upon his personal actions than in the speech delivered in his own defense, and it is most likely that the second speech would have gained little in importance had it been completed by Guicciardini.

The *Consolatoria*, *Oratio Accusatoria*, and the *Oratio Defensoria* are minor works, far less important in the development of Guicciardini's political and historical thought than are his earlier discourses and dialogues. They are essentially biographical documents akin to the earlier *Ricordanze*. However, they do have a bearing on the philosophical attitude reflected in the *Ricordi.* Guicciardini began collecting his maxims as early as 1512 - 1513 and completed the final version only in 1530. Several of the key ideas expressed in the *Ricordi,* particularly the emphasis upon the limitations of human reason and the bittersweet rewards of worldly success, first appear in the *Consolatoria.* In this respect, the work is similar to the *Dialogue on the Government of Florence* in its anticipation of ideas later expressed in a more rigorously philosophical framework. The separation of the *Ricordi* from these minor works is thus more a matter of convenience for the scholar than a reflection of the continuous ongoing process of contemplation and reflection that eventually produced the final version of that work. The fact that Guicciardini chooses the form of paired speeches, each reflecting and developing a separate and conflicting viewpoint, is not simply a part of the intellectual baggage of the legal profession. It also demonstrates that Guicciardini's particular approach to intellectual problems demands dialectical argumentation and the consideration of all aspects of a complex problem. It is a method used in the earlier *Dialogue on the Government of Florence* to present an original solution for Florence's constitutional problems. It is also a classical stylistic device employed by many humanist historiographers of the Italian Renaissance, a device Guicciardini reuses in the many paired speeches delivered by characters in *The History of Italy.* Unfortunately, in the *Oratio Accusatoria* and *Oratio Defensoria,* Guicciardini never succeeds in transcending the artificiality of an intellectual exercise or a lawyer's game. Guicciardini's vision was clearest when it scanned broader horizons, for his skill in combining all the particular and seemingly disconnected details of an historical or political event into an exciting panorama is unequaled in Renaissance historiography. Unlike either Machiavelli, Montaigne, or Cellini, Guicciardini's vision of his own personality lacked both a philosophical framework and the proper form of egotism to transform the description of his personality into a more universal expression of the human spirit. Guicciardini's private monologue in these works thus concludes with no real development beyond the important, yet philosophically limited, achievements of the political discourses and dialogues. His subsequent dialogue with his contemporary Niccolò Machiavelli, however, would provide the intellectual stimulus and the dialectic his keen mind seemed to demand to bring forth a work of great merit.

CHAPTER 5

Guicciardini and Machiavelli

A comparison of Guicciardini and Machiavelli is almost obligatory in any discussion of the Italian Renaissance. Perhaps no other two thinkers of the period have either fascinated or repelled so many readers as these two Florentines, so alike in their intellectual power and yet so different in personality and perspective. Guicciardini was the first important political thinker to respond to the appeal of Machiavelli's ideas with a work that remained unknown until the nineteenth century, a book now known as *Considerations on the 'Discourses' of Machiavelli*. The work was composed during 1530, after Guicciardini left Florence for the court of Pope Clement VII to escape the persecution of the radicals then in control of the Florentine Republic. Machiavelli's *Discourses* became available to the public four years after the author's death in 1527, but Guicciardini apparently had access to the autograph manuscript finally published in Rome by Blado in 1531. His work is thus a gloss of another gloss, a commentary on a commentary, for Machiavelli's treatise was also a series of essays based upon observations on historical events reported by the Roman historian Livy in his description of republican Rome.

Guicciardini's manuscript remains incomplete, with commentary upon thirty-eight chapters and the introduction to Book Two out of a total of 142 chapters and two introductions. He apparently intended to discuss other aspects of Machiavelli's work, since the autograph manuscript of Guicciardini's commentary lists an additional twenty consecutive chapters still to be glossed. These pages, however, remained blank after the work was once abandoned. The reason for this abandonment of a work in progress is not easily determined. Guicciardini's biographer suggests that the reasons may have been several — lack of time, simple weariness and pressing personal problems, or a dearth of observations deemed worth the expense of further intellectual effort.[1] It is most likely that Guicciardini realized the work represented no progress beyond the ideas expressed in his earlier dialogues and discourses. He was not lacking in imagination during this period, for he also completed the final version of the more important *Ricordi* during that same year.

I *The* Considerations: *A Time for Reassessment*

The *Considerations* represent for Guicciardini an opportunity to reassess his positions on a number of important issues, political problems expressed and discussed clearly and compellingly by Machiavelli. Because of its status as a commentary, the content of the work is dependent to some extent upon the opinions voiced by Machiavelli. Areas of agreement between the two men emerge, but clearly these are the parts of the work which least engage the reader today. More important and central to Guicciardini's political philosophy are his disagreements with positions taken by Machiavelli, his clarifications and modifications of certain concepts, and even his omissions. Even where Guicciardini seems to accept Machiavelli's interpretations of Livy, nuances often negate any real agreement in principle. A typical example of this sort of disagreement with Machiavelli, this habitual qualification of Machiavelli's views, is Guicciardini's acceptance of the theory that a mixed state is the best possible form of government for a republic. This argument was presented earlier by Guicciardini in the *Dialogue on the Government of Florence*, and superficially it appears that both men agree upon this fundamental problem of political organization. Nonetheless, in the *Considerations*, Guicciardini's attacks upon Machiavelli's definition of the term "people" make it apparent that each man had a divergent concept of what a mixed government would actually be in practice. Unlike Machiavelli, who placed great faith in the people, especially in the Florentines, Guicciardini, notwithstanding his pessimistic remarks about man's innately weak nature, viewed any mixed government as essentially a facade behind which the aristocratic elite, the most prudent and wise men of the city, would govern with as little interference from other classes as possible. Thus, Guicciardini remains true to those beliefs expressed in his first historical work written several decades earlier.

Guicciardini also seems to agree with Machiavelli when the latter remarks in his introduction to the second book of the *Discourses* that contemporaries often praise antiquity too highly and often deprecate their own age for no good reason. Nonetheless, the implications of this belief are radically different in the works of each writer. Machiavelli meant to demonstrate that although the great heroes of the past were exemplary models to be followed in all political affairs, they were nevertheless only men like the Italians of his day. In Machiavelli's *Discourses*, the warning not to overestimate the perfection of the classical period of Rome was intended to spur men of his era on in their efforts to emulate, imitate, and finally to surpass the ancients. Machiavelli laments the fact that the imitation of classical antiquity, accepted by all in artistic or literary matters, is completely ignored in daily affairs of state. Guicciardini passes over Machiavelli's appeal to his contemporaries to imitate the past. In fact, the denial of this central tenet of Machiavelli's political philosophy occupies an important place in the ideas expressed in both his *Considerations* and the *Ricordi*. The only concession to the possibility of a modern rebirth of ancient excellence on Guicciardini's part is his reference to the obvious flourishing of the arts in Italy at the time: "Who does not know to what heights painting and sculpture rose in the age of the Greeks, and then the Romans, and into what neglect they subsequently fell all over the world, and how, after having been buried for many centuries they returned to life about a hundred and fifty to two hundred years ago?"[2] Even this admission, however, is set in the distant past, although Guicciardini was surely aware of the many Florentine masters around him during this period. Moreover, no moral lesson is derived from this statement of fact, no exhortation to imitate the ancients in political affairs issues forth. The optimistic fervor of Machiavelli's vision of a rebirth of Roman *virtù*, the poetic dream of a political renaissance to complement that in the arts, is completely absent.

Guicciardini's concurrence with ideas he encounters in the *Discourses* sometimes conceals basic theoretical differences between the two writers. Although Guicciardini's theories may be the less appealing, they may also reveal a deeper penetration into the reality of the political events both men witness and evaluate. The best example of his bent for practical political judgments is Guicciardini's evaluation of the place of the church in Italian politics. Machiavelli's opposition to the church as a political, although not a religious, institution is clear. Apart from the usual anticlericalism inherited from a long medieval tradition ("the nearer people are to the Church of Rome, which is the head of our religion, the less religious are they"), there is the more serious charge that "the Church has kept and still keeps our country divided . . . not having been powerful enough to be able to master all Italy, nor having permitted any other power to do so." Machiavelli sees the Roman pontiff as "the cause why Italy has never been able to unite under one head, but has always remained under a number of princes and lords, which occasioned her so many dissensions and so much weakness that she became a prey not only to the powerful barbarians, but of whoever chose to assail her."[3]

Guicciardini admits that the Roman court is a disgrace: "One can never speak ill enough of the Roman court, for it is an infamy, a pattern of all the opprobrium and vituperation of the world."[4] He further agrees with Machiavelli's view that the Church has prevented the unification of Italy under the rule of one prince or one city. But Guicciardini, closely linked to the traditions of the autonomous city-state by both his aristocratic origins and his personal inclinations, is not convinced that such unification would have been beneficial for Italy. If the unity were accomplished under a republic such as Florence or Venice, it would have surely exalted one city or region over the others, as was Florence's common practice when it acquired a formerly free territory. Unification under a king or prince, such as occurred in France, might have avoided this regional favoritism, but Guicciardini believes that Italians by nature have always rejected the monarchical form of government as unsuitable to their temperaments. Most importantly, Guicciardini observes that even if political disunity has often placed Italy in a situation of weakness, "nevertheless in all these periods she has had so many more flourishing cities than she could have had under a single republic, that I think unification would have been more unfortunate than fortunate for her."[5] Even the casual tourist to Italy can attest to the validity of Guicciardini's observation. The splendor and the cultural achievements of the diverse courts at Ferrara, Urbino, Milan, Venice, Florence, Rome, and Naples testify even today to the cultural superiority of Renaissance Italy, purchased, it now seems, at the price of failure to unify Italy into an effective European state.

Both Machiavelli and Guicciardini wanted an Italy freed from the "barbarians." Machiavelli's concluding exhortation in *The Prince* makes this plea in such an eloquent fashion that nineteenth-century Italian poets and patriots were to see in him a precursor of the *Risorgimento*. *The Prince* was written at a particular historical moment which saw a Medici pope in Rome (Leo X) and a member of the same family in control of Florence (Lorenzo, Duke of Urbino). The stage was therefore set for the establishment of a strong, stable state in central Italy backed by papal power. The Medici had, for a fleeting moment, the same opportunity that Pope Alexander VI and his son Cesare Borgia possessed some years earlier but failed to exploit completely. Although we should resist the facile temptation to view Machiavelli's conception of a unified Italy as the equivalent of nineteenth-century nationalist views, it is nevertheless true that Machiavelli did hope for a united front of like-minded Italian city-states as a barrier to further foreign incursions into Italy. Furthermore, his *Discourses* present the Roman Republic as a model for those republics, like Florence, which sought to combine republican government at home with a growing empire abroad. Machiavelli's goal for Florence was presumably expansion into the rest of the Italian peninsula, and his means would most likely have been the kind of citizen army which finally did replace the mercenary or professional army during future periods of ascendant republicanism in seventeenth-century England and eighteenth-century France and America.

Guicciardini wished to see foreign invaders driven out of Italy, but there is no reason to believe that he desired this for any other reason than to restore the situation which had allowed the separate city-states before 1494 to possess a good deal of individual autonomy. Since the fate of Guicciardini's class was closely connected for such a long period to this earlier form of political organization, it is most likely that an essentially ideological motivation, and not a desire to enjoy a pluralistic flowering of the arts in various cultural centers of the peninsula, caused Guicciardini to prefer a return to what was for him, his family, and his class a political system which had its roots in the past. With such an attitude as this, it was far easier for Guicciardini to participate, albeit unwillingly, in the destruction of the Italian city-state system than it was for him to believe in the possibility of a unified Italy. The rise of a Medici principality in Florence after 1530 might at least preserve some of the ranks and privileges of his class, even if with the backing of foreign troops, it ultimately brought about fundamental changes in Florentine political organizations. We can imagine Machiavelli agreeing to sacrifice some of Florence's independence for the common cause of unifying Italy (even though it is evident that in his mind, Florence would play a major role in this unification), but Guicciardini's republicanism was too closely linked to the interests of his class to permit such a flight of the imagination. Thus, both men grounded their thinking in a kind of republicanism; but they held fundamentally different opinions over the definition of such a system and its implications for a possible unification of Italy against the invading European powers. The two finest minds in Italy were caught up in a dilemma. Who can say with certainty whether the choice of following the hopelessly impractical aspirations of a Machiavelli rather than the sober and expedient statesmanship of a Guicciardini would have changed the course of events in sixteenth-century Italy? Italians of the past century, devoted to the cause of Italian unification, were sure that a Machiavellian response to the problem would have resulted in success, and they blamed men like Guicciardini for the failure of nationalism to take root on the peninsula.

Other fundamental divergences between Machiavelli and Guicciardini are expressed more openly. The praise of ancient Rome and its source of exemplary men and deeds represented the most essential and most characteristic tenet of Machiavelli's political philosophy. This faith in the past as a guide for the present and the future is obliquely attacked several times in the *Considerations* by Guicciardini, although never as clearly or as unequivocally as in the *Ricordi*. Guicciardini finds only the military discipline of Rome worthy of imitation; her institutions, those Machiavelli represents as the model for a contemporary republic, are deemed defective and corrupt. Furthermore, ancient practices cannot be the sole guide for Renaissance men, since in some areas technology or knowledge has surpassed the ancients and has revealed ideas or inventions unknown to the past, such as gunpowder, the printing press, and the science of navigation. A second major disagreement is found in Guicciardini's more optimistic definition of human nature. As he had done in earlier works, Guicciardini maintains that human nature is essentially good but frail; it is not innately evil, as Machiavelli maintains, or as the Augustinian strain of medieval philosophy had always proclaimed. One suspects, however, that Guicciardini refers to men of his own particular social class when he writes in such a manner; for he lacks Machiavelli's faith in the people as the cornerstone of a good republican government, a faith maintained throughout the *Discourses*, and his enumeration of popular vices and shortcomings is in clear contrast to his statement that men, in general, are good.

II   *Ideological Prejudices and Popular Government*

When he rejects Machiavelli's praise of the popular element in a mixed government, Guicciardini's ideological prejudices stand out most clearly. His constant predilection for the aristocracy is sharpened by a certain bitterness and a personal resentment which expresses itself in many references to the current misconduct of the Florentine Republic toward Guicciardini and certain members of the patrician class suspected of sympathy for the exiled Medici. Guicciardini disagrees with Machiavelli that the people are more grateful than princes; in his own experience, the opposite had been the case. In his opinion, the common citizens scorn "other citizens higher than themselves and they always want to pull them down," while a prince has nothing to fear from his inferiors.[6] The aristocrats supply the element of prudence essential to all serious matters of state. In Guicciardini's model republic, the people would not have any voice in important matters and would be allowed absolutely no free debate over legislation presented for their approval or rejection. Guicciardini describes the people as "a treasury of ignorance and confusion." Moreover, this segment of the populace is often deceived; since the people "believes false rumours, it acts from frivolous motives, and in fact its ignorance is much more dangerous than the decisions of a few may be."[7] Elsewhere, Guicciardini's criticism of popular government almost takes the form of a list of those affronts for which he never forgave his own republican government. False accusations are termed "natural" in any free city. Guicciardini also maintains that Florentine patricians were forced to choose between the anarchy of a radical republic which had replaced the Medici or the Medici tyranny and injustice. In another bitter remark, he claims that the harsh persecution of the patricians in 1526 alienated many important citizens who might have supported a more moderate republic against the Medici. Guicciardini consistently blames the popular elements in a republic for the disunity that at the time characterized that form of government. In his *Discourses*, Machiavelli had attempted to answer such typically aristocratic objections by maintaining that social conflict was often the key to the success of the Roman state. This opinion elicits Guicciardini's indignant reply that "to praise disunity is like praising a sick man's disease because of the virtues of the remedy applied to it."[8] The place of the people in a well-ordered republic is thus a question upon which Guicciardini completely disagreed with Machiavelli for ideological, philosophical, and personal reasons.

The omissions in Guicciardini's commentary upon Machiavelli's *Discourses* are perhaps as revealing as his disagreements or qualifications. Guicciardini often comments on only one aspect of a chapter which appeals to his particular interests, ignoring a more crucial theoretical problem suggested by Machiavelli. In the second chapter of the first book of the *Discourses*, for instance, Machiavelli introduced not only his definition of a mixed government derived from Polybius and other classical theorists, but also his own particular explanation of the origin of civil society in a kind of social-contract which later found a place in the works of Hobbes, Locke, and Rousseau. Machiavelli further elucidates his own view that a principle of corruption or degeneration is operative within all human affairs, so that good governments degenerate into defective ones over a period of time and periodically require the strength and *virtù* of a reformer in order to bring them back to their first principles. The chapter is thus not only a part of a traditional debate on the nature of political organizations and their origins but is also an example of the higher level of abstraction that characterizes all of Machiavelli's works. Guicciardini responds only to the reference to a mixed government, since that had already attracted his attention in previous works. He never seriously enters into a dialogue with Machiavelli on the more important theoretical questions raised by the chapter in question. His own concept of a mixed government is highly ideological in nature and represents primarily a class judgment.

The contrast between the approaches of the two theorists is even more marked in their discussions of the place of religion and religious institutions in a polity. Machiavelli judges religion from a purely pragmatic point of view, remarking that it often served the Romans as a means of strengthening respect for law and established authority, thus helping to preserve order in the Roman Republic. In short, Machiavelli considers religion as an arm of the state. Numa, the legendary founder of the Roman religion, is thus placed on an equal level with Romulus, the founder of the Roman *polis*. Guicciardini completely avoids the commentary on this chapter, one which would have been of great interest to most other Italians of the period, because the Papal States occupied a place of crucial importance in the politics of the Italian peninsula. Guicciardini remarks only upon the less important following chapter which describes how the Romans often cynically interpreted omens in a manner which would suit their immediate military or political purposes.

The *Considerations* thus do not go far beyond the theoretical positions expressed in the earlier *Dialogue on the Government of Florence*, even though they represent one of the first, and perhaps the most interesting, chapters in the long history of European reactions to Machiavelli's political theories. One critic has implied that "coherent Machiavellianism becomes Guicciardinianism,"[9] but coherency is found only in the *Discourses* of Machiavelli and not in Guicciardini's *Considerations*. A systematic political theory, a presentation of interrelated ideas organized, illustrated, and dominated by certain basic and well-defined principles can be deduced from Machiavelli's *Discourses*. Furthermore, Machiavelli's commentary on Livy, although founded upon an admiration for the past and a disdain for many practices of his contemporaries, is a plan for future action. It is not a work of passive or disinterested contemplation but rather a poetic call to arms. Perhaps because he knew the limitations of human possibilities all too well from personal experience, Guicciardini lacks, at this point in his intellectual development, the faith in the possibility of constructive, dynamic political action that animates the pages of Machiavelli's works. Even when Guicciardini's observations are reflective of a fuller comprehension of the same events discussed by Machiavelli, his viewpoint is essentially conservative. As Ridolfi puts it, "he who knew how to see his friend's weak points with such marvelous acuity, had not observed that all those errors are merely rough stones on the surface of new roads opened up by his thought."[10] Guicciardini's commentary on Machiavelli is limited not by the author's intellect but by his refusal, in his attention to smaller details, to deal with the basic theoretical questions raised by Machiavelli.

Guicciardini's explanations are the type that paralyzes effective practical action, whereas Machiavelli's insights are capable of galvanizing the spirit and energy of the reader in spite of their logical inconsistencies or factual errors. An essentially poetic thinker, Machiavelli characteristically dresses his thought in a dramatic, polemical, antithetical style based upon sharp polarities and stark contrasts. The vigor of his mind and his absolute faith in the possibility of morally redemptive political action thus finds a felicitous medium of expression in his self-assured, often overconfident assertions which frequently admit of no qualification or exception. This Promethean stance is no longer possible for Guicciardini, since his own experience in public life as well as his philosophical pessimism about the possibilities of human reason lent no credence to such a faith in the future. His qualifications and his exceptions usually strike their target with great accuracy, but it is this quality that at the same time vitiates the content of the work as a guide to human behavior outside the realm of theoretical contemplation. The works of Machiavelli and Guicciardini exemplify both the virtues and defects of a highly imaginative deductive political theory, on the one hand, and a carefully expressed but narrowly conceived empiricism on the other.

III *Personal Friendship and Correspondence*

The relationship between Machiavelli and Guicciardini is not confined to Guicciardini's commentary upon the *Discourses*. Although Machiavelli was a faithful servant of Piero Soderini, the leader of the republic that Guicciardini disliked and the enemy of the Medici interests he had always served, fate decreed that the two men should become fast friends. When Guicciardini had gone to Spain early in his career as ambassador of the Florentine Republic, he would have received his instructions from The Ten of War, whose secretary was at that time Niccolò Machiavelli. There is no evidence, however, that Guicciardini was personally acquainted with Machiavelli at that time. As far as we can tell, Guicciardini first met Machiavelli in Modena in 1521 while he was governor of that town. Machiavelli had been sent on a minor mission to a meeting of the Minor Friars at Carpi and had also been entrusted with the task of finding a Lenten preacher for one of the Florentine guilds. It seems that an immediate friendship sprang up between the two men at that time. Certainly, this relationship was initially more important to Machiavelli, who, because of his association with Soderini, was still without any position of importance in the Florentine government. In contrast to Machiavelli's bad fortune, Guicciardini was the honored friend and servant of the very Medici family that had forced Machiavelli out of the government of the republic and had even had him put on the rack for a time. The letters Guicciardini found time to send to Machiavelli during his busy moments as governor show us an aspect of his character that the haughty patrician never revealed to any other of his contemporaries.

After Machiavelli left Modena, Guicciardini sent a letter to him imbued with his anticlerical opinions. The governor warns

Machiavelli not to stay in Carpi too long, or he will risk becoming both a liar and a hypocrite because of the influence of the monks. He also adds humorously that sending Machiavelli to find a virtuous preacher is as sensible as having a notorious homosexual arrange a good marriage. Machiavelli replies to the governor of Modena in a brilliant letter conceived, he claims, while sitting on the toilet considering the "extravagances" of the world. Machiavelli affirms his desire to find a good preacher for Florence, but he hopes to locate one of his own choosing, a priest who will combine all those vices in one man that the Florentines have experienced in many, a priest who will show the Florentines how to go to the devil instead of being put on the road to salvation. Machiavelli solicits Guicciardini's assistance in playing a joke on the gullible friars which will not only give both men a laugh at the church's expense but will also improve Machiavelli's prestige (and therefore the quality of his meals and lodging) among the churchmen. Machiavelli proposes that the governor periodically send him fictitious messages delivered by an official courier instructed to arrive in great haste.

Guicciardini was happy to oblige his new friend, and the joke was a great success. Machiavelli's standard of living improved, and the friars were flattered to receive a confidant of such an important official of the church. Machiavelli's host, the chancellor of the lord of Carpi, began to have doubts about the authenticity of Machiavelli's letters from Guicciardini, and the two men were finally forced to cease their fictitious correspondence in order to remain undiscovered. One letter from Guicciardini during Machiavelli's stay in Carpi is perhaps the most touching of the entire collection of letters which testifies to their close friendship. Machiavelli was a man of great courage, and although the tragic fall of the republic he had served until 1512 hurt him both professionally and personally, he called up a reserve of philosophical strength and humor in order to accept the turn of events which had deposed him from the chancellery of the republic and had placed him on a useless mission to a band of motley friars. Because his only ambition was to serve Florence, Machiavelli accepted this humiliation without a word of protest. Guicciardini, however, was more sensitive to affronts to his honor. Perhaps he saw in Machiavelli's sad treatment the portents of his own misfortunes in the future, for surely the fall of such a clever man as Machiavelli must have forced him to consider the mutability of worldly prestige and power. Guicciardini's poignant words of con-

solation to his friend seem to refer to an idea expressed many times
by Machiavelli's own *Discourses:*

My dear Machiavelli. When I read your titles of orator of the republic to the
Minor Friars and I consider with how many kings, dukes, and princes you
have negotiated in other times, I recall Lysander to whom, after so many
victories and triumphs, was given the task of passing out rations to those
same soldiers that he had formerly commanded gloriously. And I say: see
how the same events repeat themselves, the faces of the protagonists and the
superficial appearances only having changed. Nor does any unimportant
aspect of events occur that has not been seen in former times. But the fact
that the names and the appearances of things change makes it possible for
only prudent men to recognize them: and thus history is good and useful, for
it places these things before you and makes you recognize them and to see
again that which you have never known or seen.[11]

This belief in an eternal repetition of human affairs is the cornerstone of the doctrine of imitation proposed by Machiavelli in the
Discourses and *The Prince.* Here, Guicciardini admits that prudent
men can learn from the past and can profit from its example. The
reference to a classical *exemplum* is a typically Machiavellian
technique. In the *Ricordi*, however, and to a lesser extent in the
Considerations, Guicciardini is less optimistic about the possibilities
of a didactic application of human history.

The Carpi experience sealed a friendship which deepened and
continued until Machiavelli's death in 1527. All the letters that must
have passed between the two men have not been preserved, but
what time has not effaced reveals a close bond of mutual affection
and intellectual respect which still honors the memories of both
men. The content of this correspondence ranges over a wide field of
subjects. Several letters discuss the affections of various courtesans
for Machiavelli and show us that the proud governor of Modena was
himself easy prey for a pretty face. In others, Machiavelli reports on
properties acquired by Guicciardini and tells of his efforts to arrange
a marriage between one of Guicciardini's daughters and a member
of the influential Strozzi family. In the midst of the composition of
his own *History of Florence* which had been commissioned by Pope
Clement, Machiavelli declares that he would be willing to pay a
goodly sum of money to have his friend by his side when, having to
come to "certain particular facts," he has to deal with the problem
of describing his Medici patrons without flattery or offense to
historical truth.[12] Machiavelli thus acknowledges Guicciar-

dini's unique grasp of historical details which would finally bear fruit in *The History of Italy.* One letter from Machiavelli to his friend even contains a recipe for a purge to relieve Guicciardini of an uncomfortable condition which often plagued him. After the popular triumph of Machiavelli's comedy *Mandragola* in Venice, Guicciardini offered to present the work at the carnival of Modena in 1526, not just because of the work's merit but, as he admits, because it would force Machiavelli to visit him again. In another letter, Machiavelli quotes from Dante, citing from memory, as was his frequent practice with the many poets he knew so well. Never a match for his friend's erudition, Guicciardini complains in his reply: "you have made me search all over Romagna for a copy of Dante . . . and I finally found the text, but there was no commentary. I think that this is just one of those tricks that you usually have up your sleeve!"[13]

Their affection was thus genuine and deep in spite of the differences which separated them in their past actions, their social origins, and their intellectual viewpoints. Machiavelli wrote to Francesco Vettori, "I love Messer Francesco Guicciardini, I love my native land more than my soul,"[14] thus linking the deep admiration he felt for his new friend to that boundless love he had for Florence. After the initial letters to Carpi, Guicciardini consistently addressed Machiavelli by the title "honored as a brother" and even complains in one instance that Machiavelli uses too many titles in his letters to him, warning that he will begin to fill his own correspondence with grandiose titles if Machiavelli does not immediately cease the practice. This request to terminate certain formalities from a man who valued such emblems of his prestige above everything else save his honor is no small tribute to the esteem in which he held Machiavelli. In a letter addressed to Roberto Acciaiuoli, Guicciardini describes Machiavelli's unsuccessful efforts to organize a national militia for the League of Cognac before the disastrous sack of Rome: "Machiavelli is here. He had come to reorganize this militia, but seeing how corrupt it is, he is not confident they will do him credit. He will stay to laugh at human error since he cannot remedy it."[15] Guicciardini, unlike Machiavelli, would live long enough to witness and describe in *The History of Italy* the tragic results of this comedy *all'italiana.* His brief portrait of Machiavelli's intellectual attitude during the period when Italy's independence was being destroyed reveals both a deep understanding of Machiavelli's personality and, perhaps, an admiration for the peace of mind that Machiavelli's sense of humor allowed him, a method of maintaining psychological equilibrium in the face of personal disappointments which Guicciardini was later to adopt himself.

The letters of Guicciardini and Machiavelli represent an indispensable element in our understanding of Guicciardini's personality and his works. Without them, we might be tempted to believe the generations of commentators and critics who attacked Francesco Guicciardini's personality; and we might accept the picture Francesco De Sanctis painted of the "Guicciardinian man" devoid of all humanity or sentiment. Guicciardini's friendship and esteem for Machiavelli does him great honor. Not only was he one of the first major European thinkers to respond to the intellectual power of Machiavelli's works in his *Considerations*, but he also opened up his own personality to reveal a dimension of himself to Machiavelli that was never perceived by his contemporaries. Under the harsh exterior of Guicciardini's public character, Machiavelli's intellect and enthusiasm uncovered a human being who had refused any literary dialogue with his time and whose innermost thoughts (with the exception of *The History of Italy*) were closed to even his closest relatives and associates. For such a warm, open, generous person as Machiavelli to declare that he loved Guicciardini as much as his native city and both more than his own soul is a tribute that perhaps only Guicciardini, who loved Florence even more than his personal honor, could fully appreciate.

CHAPTER 6

Guicciardini's Ricordi

NONE of Guicciardini's early works was ever meant either to be published or to be perused even by a large literary audience. We can but speculate upon the reasons why Guicciardini did not have any or all of them printed. His *Ricordi*, which compares with *The History of Italy* in intrinsic interest, if not in its impact upon modern thought, appeared in an unauthorized version during the Renaissance shortly after Guicciardini's death. One of the copies of a manuscript comprised of a series of maxims or reflections on a variety of subjects was given away as a gift by one of the Guicciardini family around 1561, and it appeared in print fifteen years later in Paris; another edition was issued in Venice in 1582.[1] These editions served as the basis for numerous translations in many languages.[2] When the Guicciardini family archives were finally examined in detail in the last century by Giuseppe Canestrini, two autograph manuscripts of this work were discovered labeled by Canestrini, not Guicciardini, as *Ricordi civili e politici*, or *Political and Civil Maxims;* the discovery brought about a scholarly controversy concerning the manuscript tradition of these maxims.[3] In Italian, the word *ricordi* refers to memories, recollections, or remembrances, but in this context it is best translated as "maxims." Canestrini's improvised title, however, underlines very well the fact that Guicciardini's maxims originated from his own personal experience recalled and reworked constantly over a period of eighteen years as daily affairs influenced the various versions Guicciardini wrote. The term *ricordi* also avoids the implication of the Italian *massima* (the equivalent of the English "maxim") that Guicciardini's maxims were fixed rules of conduct. As we shall discover, Guicciardini never considered them to be immutable principles of human behavior. Exceptions, nuances, and qualifications were an integral part of his personal and social philosophy as we find it contained in the thoughts he grouped together in this masterpiece.

A brief consideration of the history of the composition of these *ricordi* as modern scholarship has reconstructed it reveals the care and the continuous interest Guicciardini took in these sententious observations.[4] Guicciardini began writing his maxims during his stay in Spain in 1512. Two notebooks in his hand from that period have been conserved in the Guicciardini family archives: Q^1, containing twelve *ricordi*; and Q^2, containing twenty-nine *ricordi* (the original twelve plus seventeen others). A more comprehensive autograph manuscript, known to scholars as B, is contained in the same archives; it contains 181 *ricordi*, 171 of which were written before 1525 plus an additional ten added in April of that year. Manuscript B retains the twenty-nine *ricordi* of Q^2 in their original order. Manuscript A is no longer in existence, although most Guicciardini scholars feel it did exist and that a study of sixteenth-century versions of the *Ricordi* confirms its authenticity. Manuscript A would therefore be a version of the one given away in 1561 by a member of the family. The final version, Manuscript C, dates from 1530 and contains 221 *ricordi*, ninety-one of which are completely new and not included in Manuscript B. Many others derive from Manuscript B, but they have been revised or completely rewritten and rearranged. Like Q^1, Q^2 and B, Manuscript C, the definitive version of the *Ricordi*, is located in the Guicciardini family archives in autograph form.[5]

This complicated history of composition makes it obvious that the *Ricordi* occupied a central place in Guicciardini's thinking from his initial entrance into political life until 1530, a total of eighteen years. One may argue that this work is of secondary importance when compared to *The History of Italy*, composed between 1534 and 1540, but the fact remains, nevertheless, that this collection of reflections and maxims attracted Guicciardini's attention three times as long as the six years it required for him to compose his great history. Many of the key ideas in the *Ricordi* reflect central aspects of the earlier works discussed in previous chapters, since Guicciardini completed them while he continuously revised his *Ricordi*. Many Guicciardini scholars, however, have preferred to examine the maxims in isolation from these minor works and have often made exaggerated claims for their originality and their uniqueness in the Guicciardini canon. No such claims need to be made to warrant current interest in these fascinating observations, and it would indeed be surprising if such thoughts did not reflect the cumulative experience of Guicciardini's other writings, his private thoughts, and his views on a life spent in public service.

I *The* Ricordi *and Earlier Works*

A few examples will suffice to illustrate the underlying continuity of many ideas contained in the various versions of the collection. One of Guicciardini's key concepts is his assertion that human nature is not essentially bad, as Machiavelli had maintained, but that it is basically good, although too weak to withstand the pressures of self-interest. Both the *Discourse of Logrogno* and the *Dialogue on the Government of Florence* had proposed this principle. In the various versions of the *Ricordi*, this same idea recurs in each extant collection (Q^2 - 4, B - 3, C - 134). Another key tenet of his political philosophy was his positivistic assertion in the early dialogues that law is nothing but legitimate violence and has no morally redemptive features, no transcendental potential to transform the ethics of members of society. This seemingly cynical point of view included the corollary that men preach love of liberty but actually prefer equal treatment rather than true liberty, since the former puts all men on the same footing and abolishes special advantages that might come about because of natural ability and complete freedom of action. Each of these ideas is postulated in *ricordi* of the B and C collection (B - 95, B - 156; C - 121, C - 140). Despite their differing literary presentation, these maxims and the political treatises in discourse or dialogue form thus have certain aspects of their content in common.

At the heart of Guicciardini's thinking in this work is his rejection of all abstract schemes for the organization of human behavior, "imagined republics and principalities," as Machiavelli commented in *The Prince*, "which have never been seen or known to exist in reality."[6] Much of classical and medieval political speculation had been based upon an implicit belief that political behavior ought to be studied in terms of abstract or ideal models; less attention was normally given to empirical analyses of existing governments. Machiavelli had insisted upon a return to a less abstract form of political inquiry in his often shocking assertions that a prince who would survive should mind what the world does, not what morality preaches that it should do. But if Machiavelli had advanced the cause of realism in his attack upon thinkers who might be classified as utopian, he too had a blind spot in his thinking. Machiavelli had elevated the exemplary deeds of such successful soldiers of fortune as Cesare Borgia and Castruccio Castracani to a level of intellectual respectability and to a place of equality with ancient models of conduct. Real political behavior could therefore serve the philosopher as easily as could an abstract scheme or an ideal republic on paper. But at the same time, Machiavelli embraced the early Renaissance concept of imitation of the ancients in a more radical fashion than most other philosophers or artists of the period. Not content with following classical precedents in the arts or letters, Machiavelli wished to emulate classical deeds (particularly those described in Livy) and to bring about a rebirth of classical *virtù* in the modern world.

Guicciardini reacts to this grandiose proposal with the predictable skepticism of a man who has seen so many of his own schemes collapse under the impact of unpredictable historical change. His first encounter with Machiavelli's thought in his *Considerations on the 'Discourses' of Machiavelli* was crucial to his intellectual development, but the immediate product of his response to Machiavelli was an unfinished commentary which was markedly inferior to Machiavelli's in sophistication of argumentation or in systematic presentation of a coherent political theory. It is most likely that Guicciardini discovered during the composition of the *Considerations* that what he had to say in his dialogue with his Florentine friend could best be said outside the framework of a commentary. The importance of the *Considerations* increases when it is considered together with the *Ricordi*, since it was the first work which forced Guicciardini to crystallize his own viewpoint on the many basic theoretical issues that he had only partially examined in his commentary. It is understandable therefore, that when Guicciardini completed the final version of these maxims, he left the *Considerations* unfinished. His *ricordi*, in a sense, represent the completed *Considerations*.

The most explicit attack by Guicciardini on Machiavelli and the kind of thinking he represents is contained in a maxim which treats of the value of the Romans as models for the modern man: "How wrong it is to cite the Romans at every turn. For any comparison to be valid, it would be necessary to have a city with conditions like theirs, and then to govern it according to their example. In the case of a city with different qualities, the comparison is as much out of order as it would be to expect a jackass to race like a horse" (C - 110).[7]

Not only are the specific Roman models impossible to follow, but the method of following any model itself is suspect unless every particular is repeated: "To judge by example is very misleading. Unless they are similar in every respect, examples are useless, since every tiny difference in the case may be a cause of great variations in the effects. And to discern these tiny differences takes a good and perspicacious eye" (C - 117).[8] The use of classical or contemporary models is thus made almost theoretically impossible, although it may be possible, Guicciardini admits, for a wise man to glimpse dimly for a brief moment some order behind the chaos of events. This can be done, however, only with the greatest difficulty and never with a guarantee of success. It is certainly not possible for anyone but the most extraordinary of men.

To this theoretical objection Guicciardini adds a more practical and a more convincing one. For him, the imitation of the past or of the present is an impractical goal because we lack reliable, complete, unbiased information upon which to base our actions. All historians, Guicciardini notes, "without exception have erred in leaving out of their writings many facts well known to their contemporaries, simply because they presupposed everyone knew them. That is why we now lack information on so many points in Roman, Greek, and all other history" (C - 143).[9] This empirical concern over our knowledge of the past is, in Guicciardini, broadened to include knowledge of the present as well. Furthermore, his pessimistic nature causes him to doubt sure knowledge of any historical fact:

You need not be surprised at our ignorance of things that happened in past ages, or of things that happen in the provinces and in far off places. If you think about it carefully, you will find we do not have any true information about the present or about the things that happen every day in our own city. Often there is such a dense cloud or a thick wall between the palace and the market place that the human eye is unable to penetrate it. When that is the case, the people will know as much about what the rulers are doing or the reason for doing it as they know about what is happening in India. (C - 141)[10]

When our historical knowledge of any human activity is viewed as uncompromisingly faulty and when imitation of the past is seen as impossible unless every particular is repeated in the present, the heuristic value of the Renaissance theory of imitation is destroyed. Guicciardini's assertions, if true, undermine the predictive value of the doctrine of imitation and render it useless as a theory to guide human conduct. Men who compose discourses on the future course of events based upon historical precedents will be mistaken: "The affairs of this world, therefore, cannot be judged from afar but must be judged and resolved day by day" (C - 114).[11]

II *The Rejection of Abstract Theory*

Abstract theory becomes useless, not only because it is based upon the faulty premises of the doctrine of imitation or the belief that the past or the present can be known, but also because a further difficulty is involved in transferring speculative knowledge into concrete action: "How different theory is from practice! The knowledge of such men is useless. It is like having a treasure stored in a chest without ever being able to take it out" (C - 35).[12] Only once does Guicciardini admit that repetition of events in the course of history might be possible: "Everything that has been in the past and is in the present will be in the future. But the names and appearances of things change, so that he who has not a discerning eye will not recognize them. Nor will he know what line to take or what judgment to form" (C - 76).[13] Since the discerning observer is a rarity in Guicciardini's universe, this maxim contains little that might support the optimistic Machiavellian argument for an eternal cyclical repetition of historical events. It is also interesting to note that this maxim (C - 76) alone, among the important statements on the doctrine of imitation in the final version of the work examined so far, is a version of a previously written maxim (B - 114). All the rest (C - 35, C - 110, C - 114, C - 117, C - 141, and C - 143) have no precedents in earlier versions of the *Ricordi* and represent fresh, new additions to the previous collections. They testify to a growing pessimism and a deepening belief on Guicciardini's part that the general intellectual assumptions of Machiavelli's political philosophy and also of the Italian Renaissance were faulty at the core.

Guicciardini's intellectual position is directly opposed to the humanism of the earlier Renaissance and is an integral part of what Hiram Haydn has termed the "Counter-Renaissance," a reaction against the supremacy of Reason as proposed by the predominantly Italian humanists.[14] As Joseph Mazzeo has noted, this Renaissance humanist rejected the model figure of the medieval theologian or religious sage for the artist or magician: "however different, they are both makers and doers who conceive of their very activities as acts of the understanding."[15] Even Machiavelli's ideal prince was defined in terms of an artistic impulse, for only he could mold the raw material of the Italian people into a strong state just as the artist makes clay or stone into a work of art. Men like the mythical Dr. Faustus or real individuals like Paracelsus, Leonardo da Vinci, Marsilio Ficino, and Pico della Mirandola viewed man as essentially a being whose function was to unlock the secrets of the universe by whatever method was at his disposal. Not the least of these methods was a revitalization of the accomplishments of classical antiquity. The *humanista,* originally a teacher of Latin, held the key to the secrets of the ancients by virtue of his knowledge of the only language that made them accessible.[16] It is not surprising that the earlier humanist phase of the Renaissance was a highly bookish phenomenon, and not a few humanist scholars spent sleepless nights poring over their manuscripts in order to satiate their thirst for learning just as Dr. Faustus does in Marlowe's drama. Admirable in proper measure, this thirst had the potential for intellectual arrogance, for an overreaching concentration upon man's capabilities and a corresponding underemphasis of his limitations. No one was more aware of the dangers of such erudition than was Guicciardini.

As one Italian scholar has put it, in the century par excellence of the guidebook, the treatise, or the manual, Guicciardini wrote with his maxims the anti-guide, the anti-treatise.[17] He had always been skeptical of abstract schemes or vague philosophies which seemed to have little to do with what he viewed as the real world. These thoughts began to germinate as early as the first collection of maxims (Q^2 - 12), continued in several maxims of later collections (B - 35, B - 121), and finally culminated in one of his most important remarks in the collection: "It is a great error to speak of the things of this world absolutely and indiscriminately and to deal with them, as it were, by the book. In nearly all things one must make distinctions and exceptions because of differences in their circumstances. These circumstances are not covered by one and the same rule. Nor can these distinctions and exceptions be found written in books. They must be taught by discretion" (C - 6).[18] Like Montaigne after him, Guicciardini believes that intellect alone cannot provide man with the proper tools to function in the world: for this, he also needs the fruits of experience, of practical wisdom derived from active participation in daily affairs: "Let no one trust so much in native intelligence that he believes it to be sufficient without the help of experience. No matter what his natural endowments, any man who has been in a position of responsibility will admit that experience attains many things which natural gifts alone could never attain" (C - 10).[19]

The humanists had too often believed that pure reasoning could supply all the answers man needed. Guicciardini, like Montaigne, in no way denies the usefulness of human reason in certain circumstances. But Guicciardini and Montaigne both deny that human reason is a panacea for all human problems. For Guicciardini, the primacy of reason was negated by the lack of logic in the course of human affairs, particularly that of human history.

Naturally, Guicciardini conceded that reason, along with experience, could aid the individual: "Remember this: whoever lives a life of chance will in the end find himself a victim of chance. The right way is to think, to examine, and to consider every detail carefully, even the most minute. Even if you do, it takes great pains to make things come out right. Imagine how things must go for those who drift" (C - 187).[20] Reason can guide man in leading an orderly and useful existence, but it is only one tool at man's disposal, a tool which is susceptible to many failures and shortcomings and is devoid of the semidivine attributes that had come to be associated with its use. Reason was placed below human experience as a guide to daily activity by Guicciardini, but it still remained more important than learning from books and the authority of the ancients. In a maxim discussing the legal profession (C - 208), Guicciardini criticizes lawyers for holding the authority of an ancient author above the reasoning of intelligent men of the present, comparing such an activity to the labor of a porter rather than to that of a truly educated man. Guicciardini would certainly have agreed with Montaigne that men should have their heads "well formed" rather than "full" of learning memorized without understanding. A practical man, Guicciardini believes that habit and repetition of rules of conduct might help bolster human reason and the weakness of human resolve to follow the precepts set forth in his *Ricordi*. He admits that following his maxims would be more difficult than understanding them in theory, but he suggests that "this too becomes easier if you grow so accustomed to them that they are always fresh in your memory" (C - 9).[21]

III   *The Maxim as Practical Guide*

One of the qualities of the *Ricordi* that continues to make the work attractive to the modern reader is its combination of political reflections with philosophical remarks. Unlike all of his other works, including *The History of Italy*, the observations Guicciardini offers in his *Ricordi* concerning politics or history are part of a more general philosophical point of view. His philosophy is not a systematic one, nor is it one which might be described as scholarly. Rather, it is a series of loosely interrelated ideas, expressed in maxim form, that can serve as a guide for practical living. In this sense, Guicciardini's *ricordi* served him in the same manner as the *essais* had served Montaigne to come to grips with various philosophical problems on a practical level. Guicciardini's basic attitude is one of profound skepticism concerning the efficacy of human reason. This is evident in his strictures against the doctrine of imitation or in his criticism of political theories of an abstract nature which do not include the teachings of human experience. As he puts it: "When I consider the infinite ways in which human life is subject to accident, sickness, chance, and violence, and when I consider how many things must combine during the year to produce a good harvest, nothing surprises me more than to see an old man, a good year" (C - 161).[22]

Guicciardini had always instinctively believed that human nature was not as evil as either the Christian tradition or Machiavelli had painted it, and as we have already seen, this belief is expressed in most of his earlier works and is repeated in the *Ricordi*. In the latter work, the idea takes on a more philosophical tone as many of the speculative reflections seem to provide added proof of the goodness but essential weakness of the human condition: "All men are by nature inclined towards good rather than evil. Nor is there anyone who would not rather do good than evil, unless other factors induce him to the contrary. But human nature is so fragile, and temptations are so many, that men let themselves be easily deviated from the good" (C - 134).[23] In the past, Guicciardini had placed such statements in works calculated to provide suggestions for practical change in the world of public affairs. Consequently, his accent had been on the goodness of human nature, and he believed that men could be persuaded or coerced by the proper laws and institutions into following their best instincts. In the *Ricordi*, however, the practical purpose of the idea is now overshadowed by the intellectual or contemplative intent of the maxim. As a result, Guicciardini's emphasis shifts from the optimistic possibility of reform to the more pessimistic view that human nature may be too weak to uphold any positive change.

Guicciardini goes beyond the rejection of the possibility of predicting human behavior and denies the existence of any knowable transcendental explanations in the world of man. He scorns astrology as a science which is "either completely false or else the things necessary for its practice are unknowable or unattainable by the human mind" (C - 207).[24] He attacks the belief in miracles in several places. Once, he declares that "miracles, like prophecies, are secrets of nature, the reasons for which the human intellect cannot fathom" (C - 123); again, he remarks that pleas to saints or sacred objects for certain results "are brought about more by the credulity of men than because anyone really sees their effects" (C - 123).[25] His general opinion is that "philosophers and theologians, and all those who investigate the supernatural and the invisible, say thousands of insane things. As a matter of fact, men are in the dark about such matters, and their investigation has served and serves more to exercise the intellect than to find truth" (C - 125).[26] The same "dark cloud" that separates man's understanding from the knowledge of the intimate workings of governments also divides human reason from ultimate answers about the universe. Cut off from any recourse to an ideal past, a redemptive present, or a transcendental solution in the future, man in Guicciardini's universe is left with little upon which to rely save his fallible reason, his limited experience, and his discretion. It is an imperfect world where "nearly everything contains some imperfection in all its parts. You must resolve to take things as they are, and to consider good that which has in it the least evil" (C - 126).[27] In a world where "there are more bad men than good, especially in matters regarding property or power," Guicciardini advises us not to trust anyone in spite of his remarks elsewhere that human nature is essentially good but weak (C - 201).[28] Even the superior intellect of the wise man, the man who might possess the necessary discretion and experience to survive in such a world, is cursed by virtue of his very superiority: "A superior intellect is bestowed upon men only to make them unhappy and tormented, for it does nothing but produce in them greater turmoil and anxiety than there is in more limited men" (C - 60).[29]

Such a cruel universe would have made even the normally unsqueamish Machiavelli uncomfortable. Machiavelli's world had been one based upon at least a minimum of order and calculation. Chance had a role in human affairs, but at least part of man's activities could be controlled by his own will. Guicciardini, basing his philosophical opinion primarily upon the contemporary events he had personally witnessed since 1494, was less inclined to see any order in that chaos. Since he had already denied the existence of any divine plan or any purpose in history in his other maxims, it was natural to attribute much of what happened to the power of an irrational force, Fortune: "Fortune has great power over human affairs," Guicciardini asserts, and "although cleverness and care may accomplish many things, they are nevertheless not enough" (C - 49).[30] Man's tragedy is that his best efforts based upon reason may be negated by Fortune; the wise man is often no better protected from its onslaughts than the fool: "It sometimes happens that fools do greater things than wise men. The reason is that the wise man, unless forced to do otherwise, will rely a great deal on reason and little on fortune; whereas the fool does just the opposite. And things brought about by fortune sometimes have incredible success" (C - 136).[31] The events narrated in *The History of Italy* would provide ample testimony to and empirical evidence of the accuracy of Guicciardini's more philosophical observations on the power of *fortuna* in the *Ricordi*.

This collection of maxims and sententious reflections is both a political and historical testament as well as a philosophical, personal assessment of an individual's role in the world. In an irrational universe governed by blind chance and peopled by essentially unpredictable and fallible human beings, the wise man must struggle to survive. The ambitious projects of a Machiavelli to rid Italy of "barbarians" or to build a strong, popular republic in Tuscany must give way in Guicciardini's works to more limited, more individually oriented goals. Nowhere is Guicciardini's own personal tragedy more clearly underlined than in a new maxim composed for the final version of the collection: "All cities, all states, all reigns are mortal. Everything, either by nature or by accident, ends at some time. And so a citizen who is living in the final stage of his country's existence should not feel as sorry for his country as he should for himself. What happened to his country was inevitable; but to be born at a time when such a disaster had to happen was his misfortune" (C - 189).[32] For a man of Guicciardini's talents and ambition, living during the eclipse of Florentine republicanism while the system collapsed was a great personal tragedy, particularly since his own personal interests demanded that he serve the forces that were bringing about this development. Far more preferable for him would have been a life during a time when Florence was still a major power in international and Italian affairs, a time before the rise of the powerful nation states of France and Spain which overshadowed the city - states of the Italian peninsula.

In such an era as Guicciardini's, however, the conflict between ethical principles and the practical concerns of worldly existence is increasingly evident. Codes of ethics drawn up in an earlier period come in conflict with the new modes of behavior characteristic of any period of transition. Men like Guicciardini were forced to follow courses of action which were repugnant to their basic inclinations. Guicciardini was constantly forced to sacrifice his own republican sentiments in favor of his immediate need to maintain a position of authority and influence within the church government or as an advisor of the Medici family, both of which were actively working to overturn the system so dear to him. In Guicciardini's opinion, a conflict of ethical principles and worldly matters in an era when reason and order are absent from the world cannot be resolved by a reliance upon conscience. Indeed, if the politician or the private citizen is to follow the dictates of his conscience, he and his family will surely come to ruin. Thus, the quality of discretion becomes increasingly important in human calculations. Opposed to more abstract, idealistic, or rationalistic guides to conduct, Guicciardini's *discrezione* represents, above all, the individual's ability to recognize and to follow his own private interests regardless of those of any larger entity such as the city - state or the nation. Discretion, unfortunately, is a quality that is not in ready supply. As Guicciardini notes, "if discretion is not given by nature, it can rarely be learned adequately from experience. It can never be learned from books" (C - 186).[33] Such a skill could perhaps best be translated into English as "tact" or "prudence," but the more derogatory term "expedience" is sometimes closer to Guicciardini's meaning. It certainly is a more apt description of his own personal response to a difficult period in his life, a response reflected in various entries in the *Ricordi.*

IV   *The Role of Self-Interest*

The concept of *discrezione* is therefore directly related to another key idea in Guicciardini's collection of maxims, the idea of self-interest. Self-interest, or what a critic of Guicciardini might term amoral expedience, is the only guide possible for a wise man who lives in an age of constant turmoil, an era when practical survival must, of necessity, conflict with personal morality or private conscience. Guicciardini himself lived with this contradiction throughout his public life, working for the very family and papacy that would be instrumental in destroying that Florentine social system and economic class to which his personal loyalties belonged. In Manuscript B of the maxims, he expresses his contempt for his employers succinctly: "I want to see three things before I die, but I doubt whether I shall see any of them, no matter how long I live. I want to see a well-ordered republic in our city, Italy liberated from all the barbarians, and the world delivered from the tyranny of these wicked priests" (B - 14).[34] The fervor of this remark is rather more in keeping with a tone one might expect in the works of Machiavelli than in Guicciardini. Elsewhere in the same manuscript, this estimation of the clergy is linked to Guicciardini's own employment as their servant: "Naturally, I have always wanted to see the ruin of the Papal State. But as fortune would have it, I have been forced to support and work for the power of two popes. Were it not for that, I would love Martin Luther more than myself in the hope that his sect might demolish, or at least clip the wings, of this wicked tyranny of priests" (B - 124).[35]

In the final version of Guicciardini's observations, the B - 14 maxim is entirely removed, probably because by 1530 Guicciardini saw no possibility of either another republic in Florence or the expulsion of foreign influence from the Italian peninsula. But his opinion of the temporal power of the church had not changed, nor did the Reformation that was slowly eroding papal political influence in Europe displease him entirely. The revision of B - 124 contains not only a stronger attack upon the clergy but also a most significant alteration in content, for it explains Guicciardini's employment by the church in terms of fortune's blessings and his own personal, and presumably selfish, interests:

I know of no one who loathes the ambition, the avarice, and the sensuality of the clergy more than I — both because each of these vices is hateful in itself and because each and all are hardly suited to those who profess to live a life dependent upon God. Furthermore, they are such contradictory vices that they cannot coexist in a subject unless he be very unusual indeed.

In spite of all this, the positions I have held under several popes have forced me, for my own good, to further their interests. Were it not for that, I should have loved Martin Luther as much as myself — not so that I might be free of the laws based on Christian religion as it is generally interpreted and understood; but to see this bunch of rascals get their just deserts, that is, to be either without vices or without authority. (C - 28)[36]

The implication is that for his own good ("per el particulare mio"), Guicciardini is forced to sacrifice his ideals and the demands of his own conscience. Expediency or self-interest is a force stronger than all others, and the man of *discrezione* must very often follow its dictates if he is to survive. Elsewhere, Guicciardini makes a general statement concerning success in the world: "In this world of ours, the men who do well are those who always have their own interests in mind and measure all their actions accordingly" (C - 218).[37] Nevertheless, Guicciardini asserts that not all actions taken in a man's interests are totally selfish or narrowly conceived: "But it is a great error not to know where true interest lies; that is, to think it always resides in some pecuniary advantage rather than in honor, knowing how to keep a reputation, and in a good name" (C - 218).[38] Here again, the quality of *discrezione* must play a role in helping a man determine in what direction his interests lie, and it may not be simple expediency that determines how he should act. But it must not be forgotten that the antithesis Guicciardini sees is between monetary advantage on the one hand and honor or knowing how to keep a reputation and a good name on the other. In short, self-interest need not be sacrificed as long as a man's outward reputation and the esteem of his peers is retained inviolate. But what about the hypocrisy, some would say the immorality, of a man who thinks in one manner but acts in another for "his own good"? The inward demands of conscience, as opposed to the outward requirements of society, seem to be totally ignored in Guicciardini's formulation of the problem. And it is this refusal to come to grips with the ethical issues involved in following one's own *particulare* which has aroused the ire of so many critics of Guicciardini's ideas.

Guicciardini's view of the human condition was never one tinged by sentimentality or illusions, unless we wish to categorize his failure to understand the power of moral imperatives as an illusion of the realistic variety. If his stark picture of human affairs in his maxims leaves little room for the more delicate sentiments and emotions, it also blinds Guicciardini to the power of such feelings in influencing the course of events. The first maxim in the final collection is a case in point. It is a completely new observation, one added to reflect the current events of 1530 which has no precedent in earlier collections. In it, Guicciardini discusses the nature of faith. "The pious," Guicciardini declares, "say that faith can do great things, and, as the gospel tells us, even move mountains. The reason is that faith breeds obstinacy. To have faith means simply to believe firmly — to deem almost a certainty — things that are not reasonable; or, if they are reasonable, to believe them more firmly than reason warrants. A man of faith is stubborn in his beliefs; he goes his way, undaunted and resolute, disdaining hardship and danger, ready to suffer any extremity" (C - 1).[39]

From this general theoretical observation, Guicciardini then moves to a concrete example that, he believes, proves the general theory, an analysis of the siege of republican Florence by the forces of Emperor Charles V and the exiled Medici family in 1530 which ended in the reestablishment of Medici rule and the eventual foundation of a family dynasty that would remain in power until the eighteenth century:

> In our own day, the Florentines offer an excellent example of such obstinacy. Contrary to all human reason, they prepared for an attack by the pope and the emperor, even though they had no hope of help from any quarter, were disunited, and burdened with thousands of other difficulties. And they have fought off these armies from their walls for seven months, though no one would have believed they could do it for seven days. Indeed, the Florentines have managed things in such a manner that, were they to win, no one would be surprised; whereas earlier, everyone had considered them lost. And this obstinacy is largely due to the faith that they cannot perish, according to the prediction of Brother Jerome of Ferrara. (C - 1)[40]

The power of the dictates of faith, of conscience, of a higher law than that imposed by practical necessity is lost upon Guicciardini much as the moral message of a preacher and reformer like Savonarola (here called Brother Jerome by Guicciardini) was incomprehensible to Machiavelli. Even though Guicciardini had admired Savonarola the man and had praised his political acumen in the portrait he composed of the priest for his first *History of Florence*, he betrays his lack of understanding of the religious and psychological forces behind the man's influence upon his fellow Florentines in this maxim. So far removed were the actions of the embattled Florentines during the siege from the considerations dominated by Guicciardini's guiding principles of *discrezione* and *el particulare* that they seemed foolish and irrational. When the Italians of the nineteenth century turned back to their national history to find a cause for their downfall during Guicciardini's lifetime, not a few would agree with Francesco De Sanctis that Italy had perished because the *savi* or wise men like Guicciardini had outnumbered the *pazzi*, the so-called fools whose fervor had sparked the heroic Florentine resistance to the invaders.[41]

If Guicciardini's *ricordi* reveal both a startling frankness and a deep knowledge of the ways of the world as well as a blind spot to the place of ethical considerations, they also show their author to be very much aware of his own human limitations. The entire collection of maxims is colored by an elegiac sadness, a sense that the best days have indeed passed and that human possibilities have been suddenly circumscribed in a drastic manner. We have already seen how Guicciardini felt that to be born in an era of national decline was the greatest misfortune man could suffer, and it is clear that he spoke in this remark not only for himself but also for the great majority of Italians who were witnessing the political eclipse of their particular form of civilization. What could a man do when the times were out of joint, when *fortuna* seemed to have turned away from the Italian peninsula, and when the normal calculations based upon discretion and self-interest did not seem to have any meaning? Guicciardini's answer, addressed to himself in these reflections never intended for publication, was a kind of stoic acceptance tinged by a sense of the absurdity of the human condition. He seems to have viewed man's lot as a role to be performed, as a mask to be assumed for the duration of one's brief existence in this veil of tears:

In this world, no one chooses the rank into which he will be born nor the circumstances and the fate with which he will have to live. And so, before praising or censuring men, you must not look at their condition but at how they manage within it. Praise or blame must be based on their behavior, not on the state in which they find themselves. In a comedy or a tragedy we do not have higher respect for the actor who plays the part of the master or the king than for the one who plays the servant. Instead, we pay attention only to the quality of the performance. (C - 216)[42]

Such a statement would have been unthinkable from the haughty patrician who left for the court of Spain in 1512. But the years had mellowed Guicciardini and had taught him to have a more judicious perspective on the vainglories of the world. The *ricordi* thus reflect a fuller acceptance on Guicciardini's part of the lot he shared with lesser mortals. Like other men, even the aristocrat is ultimately a character in the same drama which, at times, Guicciardini might have called more correctly a farce; all the players in this drama must carry out their roles as best they know how with no ultimate superiority inherent in any of the parts.

V   *The Style of Guicciardini's Maxims*

Guicciardini rarely comments on his own literary style in any of his works. One of the *ricordi* written for the final collection, however, refers to the structure of the maxim which he chose to give form to his private political and philosophical speculations: " 'Little and good,' says the proverb. It is impossible for someone who says or writes many things not to put in a good deal of nonsense; whereas, few things can be well digested and concise" (C - 210).[43] In spite of this stated preference for brief, terse statements, the *ricordi* range from aphoristic single sentences to long paragraphs which could well be considered short essays. Consequently, it is extremely difficult to categorize them all under any single heading or stylistic attribute. Nevertheless, Guicciardini's style in this literary genre is markedly different from that which we normally associate with the style of the literary *maxime* of the French seventeenth-century master, La Rochefoucauld, or any number of lesser writers and moralists of the same period in France.[44] While the French authors rely heavily upon the resources of rhetoric for their effects and seem to delight in word plays, double entendres, antithesis, and the like, Guicciardini strives above all for clarity. Because his reflections are written for his eyes alone, there is no hint of the salon atmosphere that we find in the French works, no trace of the specialized literary language that made the literature of French classicism possible. In spite of the fact that Guicciardini could well have patterned his reflections on literary models, as he surely did when he composed the stately prose of *The History of Italy*, it seems clear that his primary purpose was lucidity of thought and expression and not polished prose or rhetorical effect. "Little and good" may have been his preference, but in the same maxim Guicciardini wonders whether "it may have been better to select the best of these *ricordi* rather than to have accumulated so much material" (C - 210).[45] He would have no doubt revised his work even more had he not begun the composition of the much more demanding *History of Italy* shortly after the completion of the 1530 revision.

As a practical statesman with a businessman's preference for few but concise words, the literary form of the maxim would naturally appeal to Guicciardini. Given his busy life as an important political figure, it was the genre best suited to a man whose writing for most of his life would be confined only to brief interludes between the pressing affairs of state. Recording such reflections also had a time-honored place in the traditions of Florentine aristocratic families, and the practice was followed by many lesser men. As is usually the case with any great writer, the form of Guicciardini's maxims indeed reveals something about his underlying assumptions. A major tactic in the rhetoric of Guicciardini's reflections is the assertion of one fact, idea, or situation, only to be followed by a qualification or a denial of this initial assertion. The pattern could be illustrated by any number of the most important maxims in the final collection, but the previously cited observation on human nature (C - 134) will suffice to illustrate the common pattern. Guicciardini first asserts that men are by nature inclined toward the good rather than toward evil. He immediately adds, however, that this inclination can be thwarted by stronger, more irresistible pressures. The qualification continues, as Guicciardini explains that human nature is also as fragile as it is good and that temptations are never lacking. As a result, men often do evil even though their nature is of a contrary bent. In a final conclusion which demonstrates the reasoning process of the *ricordi*, Guicciardini states that laws and punishments were invented to counter this defect in human nature.

The maxim as practiced by Guicciardini is therefore a kind of reasoning process which proceeds from an initial affirmation or a presentation of an idea to its qualification, or even its rejection, and a conclusion. Rather than developing a whole series of interrelated concepts, such a literary structure is an excellent method of analyzing single ideas at a time in the most detailed manner possible. Each individual maxim tends to take on an autonomous character in the final collection of 1530, and although there is an obvious continuity in point of view and method of argumentation, the reader is forced to concentrate more upon each individual concept in a single maxim than upon the sum of the various parts of the collection of observations. Thus, the form of the collection itself tends to demonstrate Guicciardini's own aversion to the abstract, more systematic political and philosophical theories of speculative thinkers. His work conveys by its form both the spirit of its author and his rejection of highly organized abstractions. Furthermore, the common tendency to qualify or to negate initially stated ideas is further testimony within the style of Guicciardini's prose to his pessimistic and critical intellectual position. Such an approach to any idea was natural to him; nothing of a theoretical nature could be accepted by him without testing it against the fruits of his experience or the power of his logic.

Thematically, there is an important change in the final form of the collection as a recent and most important study of the various versions of the maxims has demonstrated.[46] The greatest single change from the B to the C manuscript, besides the addition of ninety-one new *ricordi* and the revision of many older ones, is the method used by Guicciardini in his revisions. Over two-thirds of the *ricordi* in Manuscript C are highly speculative and theoretical; few refer to specific events or particular political institutions, and when this occurs, it is only as an illustration of a more generally applicable idea. For example, the C manuscript completely eliminates the early Q^2 *ricordi* from the opening section of the work, whereas they had been retained in their entirety in Manuscript B. And these early Q^2 remarks had a distinctly parochial flavor, a tendency to concentrate more upon specifically Florentine institutional problems and less upon more universal political or philosophical questions. The revisions shift away from clusters of *ricordi* on the same theme and focus attention upon the individual maxim itself. As a result, the final version is clearly different in tone from the other political or historical works Guicciardini had written since 1508, for in it Guicciardini is less concerned with the political problems of the moment or the necessary institutional reforms he felt were necessary for the government of his native Florence. By 1530, practical goals were increasingly impossible for Guicciardini. Abandoning any practical aim, the maxims avoid the particular political problems of the moment, problems limited in scope to the now parochial institutions of a small city-state already out of touch with the realities of the times. As Emanuella L. Scarano has noted, this predominantly theoretical tone in the *Ricordi* explains why the work, alone of Guicciardini's many political and historical writings, can be read without any previous background study in the ideas or institutions of the epoch.[47] Furthermore, the basic renunciation of practical goals for theoretical speculation we witness in the *Ricordi* underlines the modernity of this collection of reflections and joins it, in both tone and intent, to Guicciardini's final masterpiece, *The History of Italy*.

CHAPTER 7

Guicciardini and Humanist Historiography

*T*HE *History of Italy*, Guicciardini's historical masterpiece, seems to have required a whole lifetime of literary and political experience. When compared to the scope and depth of this work, his other historical writings and political dialogues almost appear to be trial runs for the one work that truly expresses his literary talents, his practical political experience, and his skill in historical narrative. *The History of Italy* was, in fact, a product of years of initial preparation, thought, and apprenticeship. His earlier attempt to write a history within the humanist tradition, entitled *Florentine Affairs*, served him as a means of perfecting a new historical methodology which places him among the founders of modern historiography. The existence of this work was discovered only in this century after it had remained undetected for almost four hundred years.

Guicciardini's innovative historical techniques grew out of a tradition of highly stylized historical works produced by Italian humanists before him. The humanist movement in scholarship and letters reached its zenith in Florence during the fifteenth century. This movement spread across the Alps to influence the whole of educated Europe, producing such diverse talents as Erasmus, Budé, Calvin, and others, and influencing countless creative writers like Rabelais, Montaigne, Spenser, and Shakespeare. Among the many humanist contributions to philology and to scholarship, the analysis of the false Donation of Constantine by Lorenzo Valla, the first translation of the works of Plato, and the discovery and publication of editions of many other classical writers are the best known. Italian humanists imparted to the European Renaissance their special view of classical Rome as the source of excellence in the arts, letters, and moral philosophy. Because of its special status, the ancient world was viewed by the humanists as the model for Renaissance man to emulate and, if possible, to surpass. Although the humanists were originally teachers of ancient languages, their conception of linguistic studies was as broad as the viewpoint of today's cultural historian and often encompassed much of what we now consider to be the domain of the humanities. It was therefore predictable that they would emphasize not only the content but also the literary merits of their Latin masters and that the humanistic movement would find its best literary expression not in the vernacular but in a newly revived and highly sophisticated Renaissance Latin.

I *Humanist Models and Style*

The humanists admired the Latin historians, particularly Livy, Caesar, and Sallust. In accepting these writers as models for the style and content of their own historical works, the humanists expressed at once their admiration for classical Latin prose, their interest in the great deeds of the protagonists of the past as guides for present conduct, and their contempt for the chronicles of their medieval predecessors, which were dismissed by one of their number as "base scribblings of monks."[1] History was not yet a discipline which obeyed its own rules or followed its own logic, nor was it yet practiced by professional historians established in universities. Rather, history offered the early Renaissance humanists a vast reservoir of facts, personalities, and events from which they could select those elements which especially interested them. Because these histories were regulated by the classical commonplace that history teaches by example, *per exempla docet,* moral guidance and didactic instruction were their goals. Founded upon this concept of history as a guide for present conduct, these humanist works were inevitably concerned with persuading readers to accept their lessons. Consequently, the humanists followed the classical precepts of Cicero and usually considered the field of historiography as a branch of the art of rhetoric.

In the composition of historical narrative, humanist historiography thus developed certain preferences in both subject matter and style. Because the Romans were considered to have progressed beyond the Greeks in such matters, Latin historians were most frequently chosen as models. Largely because of the influence of Livy, Caesar, and Sallust, the two subjects deemed most worthy of treatment were the history of a war or of a city - state. Certain stylistic elements in classical histories were elevated to a place of prominence. Highly wrought descriptions of battle scenes were especially esteemed. Beginning with a background treating the nature of the opposing peoples, the historian would continue his narrative by carefully describing the site of the battle as well as the omens which foretold its outcome. As might be expected in a highly rhetorical art, stylized speeches by generals to their troops or by politicians and diplomats were inserted by the humanists to call attention to the importance of a battle, the implications of a political decision, or the personality of a historical character. These speeches were usually not accurate historically but were the product of the writer's imagination. Most humanists were content to express not exactly what was said on a given occasion but what might have been said upon such an occasion, continuously maintaining an ideal, abstract, and general viewpoint in their narrative in keeping with their didactic goals. Invented speeches were often presented in pairs in order to compare contrasting points of view. Literary portraits were frequently placed within the narrative after a character's death to highlight the didactic implications of the man's deeds or personality. In the case of the humanist histories of a city - state, the discussion of the origins of the city often assumed an importance far beyond that which the modern historian might grant the subject today. It was here that the humanists most often displayed their philological prowess and their concern with the accuracy of historical sources and documents.

The methods of the humanists would be no more acceptable to the modern historian than would their didactic point of view or their rhetorical style. The insistence upon using primary documents whenever available and assessing all available evidence in the composition of a synthesis as an end product of original investigation was not felt to be especially important, although this process is the foundation of all serious historical investigation today. Humanist historians were often government officials who were composing officially commissioned works for a public or a private patron. They were employed not so much for their considerable expertise in using the available scholarly resources, but for their mastery of a literary language, usually Latin. Consequently, the collection of materials and the accounts of facts to be inserted into the final, artistic version of a work could be accomplished just as efficaciously by lesser employees of the government or assistants to the historian. Most humanists, however, seemed to agree that a source's accuracy increased to the extent that the author was nearer to the events he described. Those historians who used primary sources apparently did so not because they judged them to be more valid than secondary materials, as a modern historian would, but simply because they were more conveniently accessible. Since primary documents were not always the basis of their works, their main theoretical problem was to establish how to choose the single narrative source, usually another history, that would be followed in the treatment of a given historical event, period, or character.

II   *Historiography in Italy Before Guicciardini*

All the important city-states of Italy had humanist historians who composed various works on their native cities, expressing both a civic patriotism and a basic human desire to preserve for posterity the memory of the most outstanding citizens. Thus, Marcus Antonius Sabellicus (1436 - 1506) composed the *Decades* on the city of Venice, and his place as Venetian historiographer was later filled by Andrea Navagero (1483 - 1529) and Pietro Bembo (1470 - 1527). In Florence, there was a long tradition of humanist historical literature within that city's government. Leonardo Bruni (1369 - 1444), Poggio Bracciolini (1380 - 1459), and Bartolomeo Scala (1428 - 1497), all secretaries in the Florentine Chancellery, produced Latin histories of Florentine affairs whose inspiration was the classical work of Livy. In addition to this more learned humanist tradition centered in the chancellery, there was also a vernacular tradition which dated from the medieval period. The most important of the earlier histories cited by all historians of the Renaissance is the *Cronica* of Giovanni Villani (c. 1270 - 1348). Niccolò Machiavelli's *History of Florence* (published in 1532 after an initial circulation in manuscript form) may be seen as a bridge between the more learned humanist historiography and the vernacular works. Machiavelli was a former member of the same chancellery which produced so many Latin histories, but his own study of Florence was commissioned by the Medici and was written, like the several histories by Guicciardini, in Italian.

The fact that both Machiavelli and Guicciardini chose to write all their important historical works in Italian rather than in Latin is not without importance. The humanists had preferred the Latin language as a more dignified, noble means of expression. Many of the best known works of the European Renaissance were written in Latin — Petrarch's *Secretum*, Boccaccio's *The Fates of Illustrious Men*, Erasmus's *In Praise of Folly* and *The Education of a Christian Prince*, and Sir Thomas More's *Utopia*. The last two works were composed at roughly the same time as Machiavelli's *Prince* (1513). Histories continued to be written in Latin throughout the next several centuries in Europe, but the most important historical works written during this period in Italy were composed in Italian, and many were written by Florentines. Because the humanists had composed their narratives for a relatively small, elite audience, such histories as those of both Bruni and Bracciolini were first published in their original form in Latin only centuries later. Authorized Italian translations commissioned by the Florentine government were printed immediately, however, in the fifteenth century.[2] Thus, not only did most humanists value most highly works in Latin, but many even preferred works preserved in private manuscripts to printed copies. The choice both Guicciardini and Machiavelli made to produce histories in the vernacular must, in this light, be viewed as a conscious effort to popularize their works. Moreover, both men use the medium of a humanist literary genre to express ideas that supersede the simple desire to inculate a moral lesson. As political problems begin to occupy the historian's attention in their works, history becomes closely allied with the formulation of political theory. Guicciardini's *History of Florence* and Machiavelli's *History of Florence* present substantially more than a series of moral *exempla* to follow. Each work represents a political analysis and an assessment of the city's affairs within the framework of a historical narrative.

Although both Guicciardini and Machiavelli went beyond the limits of humanist historiography, the influence of this literary tradition was not unimportant in the formulation of their historical perspectives. The humanist emphasis upon the specific subject matter of war and the affairs of city - states caused Renaissance writers to concentrate upon political rather than cultural, economic or religious affairs. This emphasis in turn forced the historians to deal with the many practical constitutional problems of their day and, consequently, the histories often contain much of the best political thought of the period. The historians who followed the Latin humanists in the veracular inherited their belief that political activity could be guided by human reason and that society was at least partially the product of human activity, not mere chance or unfathomable divine plan. Problems of politics revealed by historical narratives of the distant past were an important means of discovering how to govern conduct in the future. Finally, the interest in the polished style and the orderly chronological arrangement of narrative which characterized the Latin histories helped Renaissance historians writing in the vernacular to avoid what they considered the rambling, disorganized, often incoherent form of the medieval chronicle.[3] By stressing the place of rhetoric or the art of persuasion in their works, the humanists helped to make history the branch of the embryonic social sciences which has to this day retained important links with literature and which has produced some of the great prose stylists in many different languages.

III   Florentine Affairs

Guicciardini's second history, *Florentine Affairs*, was begun in 1527, almost two decades after the composition of *The History of Florence*. Guicciardini returned to this work several times during his lifetime but finally left it unfinished. *Florentine Affairs* was published in its entirety only in this century, although the nineteenth-century edition of Guicciardini's works which contained the first *History of Florence* had previously published excerpts of the book without recognizing them as part of a larger history.[4] The historical period covered by both works is approximately the same. The earlier work had begun with the Ciompi revolt of 1378 and had continued to 1509, when it was suspended in mid-sentence. *Florentine Affairs* opens with a discussion of the city's origins, but the main historical narrative begins in 1375 and, as far as we can tell from the unfinished manuscripts, the work was designed to reach at least the year 1494.

Similarities between the two histories are only superficial, for *Florentine Affairs* is meant to be an authentic humanistic history and was, in effect, intended as a reconsideration of the same historical period in a manner completely different from the first work. The earlier history was closer to a medieval chronicle in its simple, unpretentious literary form, its readiness to pronounce judgments based primarily upon opinions or prejudices, and its uncritical acceptance of historical sources. The apparatus of the humanists is also present in the discourse on the city's origin, the stylized speeches sprinkled throughout the work, and the chronological arrangement of the narrative. But the rhetorical flourishes which set the work apart from the simpler *History of Florence* composed in Guicciardini's youth are not as important as are the new methods which go beyond anything found either in the

Latin works of the humanists or in the vernacular histories of the period. Guicciardini approaches his subject from a modern perspective. Instead of merely following a single source for his information on various events or characters, Guicciardini compares and evaluates all the available works on any given subject and attempts in a consistent manner to distinguish between those which are most reliable and those which are to be used only with caution. Among the historical or literary works he consults are those by Villani, Marchionne Stefani, Bruni, Bracciolini, Gino and Nero Capponi, Froissart, Piccolomini, Biondo, Sabellicus, Dante, Pliny, Tacitus, and Frontinus. This extraordinary collection of material is even more impressive if we bear in mind that much of it was still unpublished at the time and circulated privately only in manuscript form. Furthermore, but to a lesser extent than in *The History of Italy*, Guicciardini supplements such secondary works whenever possible with still unpublished primary documents or papers drawn from his own private archives.

IV *New Research Methods*

The technical aspect of the composition of this work reflects the author's innovations in historical research. He used large notebooks with wide margins in order to retain space during his writing for the notation of questions, doubts, discrepancies or conflicting sources; facts, dates, and names may be left out to be located or may be underlined for confirmation. The narrative, as it is preserved in the original manuscript in the Guicciardini family's archives in Florence, reveals an exacting attention to detail and a scrupulous search for accuracy. Guicciardini was never afraid to question a source if it seemed to be consistently biased or in conflict with other works. Of Marchionne Stefani's *Istoria fiorentina*, a work describing Florence's history until 1385 and which Guicciardini consulted in manuscript, he remarks to himself in a marginal note: "Note that Marchionne is a very faithful chronicler of the affairs of those times, that is of foreign affairs, because he worked and served as an ambassador and held offices; but in domestic affairs, he is partisan."[5] In spite of his admiration for Machiavelli, he does not frequently rely upon his friend's *History of Florence*; in one instance he even adds a marginal note to his narrative to indicate that "this passage contradicts Machiavelli."[6] The passage that disagrees with Machiavelli's work is retained, however, since it is judged to be historically accurate. In contrast to Guicciardini's careful assessment

of all available sources, Machiavelli's history had followed an un-
scholarly method much like that used in Guicciardini's first history
and was, therefore, a secondary source like so many others, not to be
preferred over any other documentary evidence at Guicciardini's
disposal.

A fair assessment of *Florentine Affairs* must take into account its
unfinished, fragmentary character. The work is nowhere near final
completion or even partial revision. It is thus not like the first
History of Florence, for even though that work is also unfinished,
what remains represents a reasonably polished, coherent, and
readable narrative. In contrast, only the first two books of *Florentine
Affairs* approach a final stage of revision. The remaining two parts
are full of lacunae which Guicciardini meant to fill in by further
research and are essentially rough drafts. Furthermore, the work was
apparently designed to include more than the four books that remain. It is the method utilized by Guicciardini in this work,
therefore, and not its content that is novel and important for the
development of a modern historiography.

One dominant thematic concern is nevertheless apparent even
from these unfinished pages. The internal strife and political rivalry
that had always plagued Florence consistently attracts the
historian's attention. After the obligatory discussion of the origins of
the city, Guicciardini immediately begins to analyze various sources
of the conflict which, as he concluded during the years 1527 - 1530,
has undermined the independence of the city in the face of foreign
incursions by the French or the Spanish. Guicciardini analyzes the
origins of civil strife in Florence and pinpoints three major sources of
discontent. There is the most ancient conflict of Guelf (the supporters of the papacy in Italy) and Ghibelline (the partisans of the
emperors). More peculiar to Florence is the conflict of the various
White and Black factions within the town. Increasingly more important in Guicciardini's day is the basic economic conflict between the
patricians and the masses. In describing this particular struggle in
his many works, Guicciardini rarely fails to reflect his aristocratic
prejudices.

The minutely precise descriptions of these separate but interrelated conflicts in the first two books of Guicciardini's *Florentine
Affairs* often remind us of his own personal political problems and
his treatment at the hands of the radical republic after the siege of
Rome had weakened Pope Clement's control of the city. An example
of such a passage is a speech delivered by Donato Barbadori in Book

Two which Guicciardini apparently viewed as one of the more important parts of his narrative; in his papers remain two other versions which were corrected and revised in order to produce the final speech inserted into this passage. Barbadori delivered the oration on 23 December 1379 before he was executed for his alleged participation in a Ghibelline plot against Florence. The accused man denied any guilt, noted that he had always served the city with distinction, and pronounced what became popularly known as the "curse of Barbadori" on his native city:

I will not speak to beg for mercy or because you may have compassion on me, knowing very well that when maliciousness rules with ignorance one cannot expect anything other than injustice and cruelty, but because at least the walls of this palace (if not the listeners) will be witnesses to my innocence, which did not suffice to save me. I should not wonder at this fact, since we have been born in a city which has always naturally hated the virtue of others and has always persecuted those who have honored or served it. What fatherland ever existed that should have recognized its salvation by one of its citizens, Farinata Uberti, who alone with his strength and goodness, prevented Florence from being razed to its very foundations? But who was ever persecuted so madly as he? . . . Dante Alighieri, outstanding man of his times, immortalized the Florentine name, and his reward was exile from his own land, he whom foreign nations esteem and adore. . . . On you, ingrateful and stupid people, I pray no other vendetta than that you may never know and never enjoy true liberty; but always living either oppressed by tyrants or, falsely thinking yourselves free in absolute anarchy, may you afflict yourselves, tear yourselves apart, and consume yourselves, always having fixed in your hearts for your torment alone the desire for liberty, since you are not capable of recognizing or using it.[7]

It is difficult not to view this speech as a reflection of Guicciardini's own personal bitterness in the light of the treatment he received before the Medici rule of Florence was reestablished in 1530. Apart from this personal note, the speech functions as an integral part of Guicciardini's portrait of the internecine conflicts which he defined as the primary cause behind the loss of both Florentine and Italian political independence during the very period when Italy achieved a cultural superiority over the rest of Europe.

Guicciardini's *Florentine Affairs* represents a revolutionary advance in historical method, a new approach to the writing of historical narrative which went far beyond the boundaries of humanist practice. The rigorous, systematic examination of historical sources in the work is a methodological innovation that compensates for the work's fragmentary condition. Ultimately, however, *Florentine Affairs* suffers from a narrow definition of subject matter. *The History of Florence,* written years earlier, although less accurate and often facile in its class-oriented political judgments, is, by comparison, a much more engaging narrative. Guicciardini's new historical method had yet to be combined with the brilliant prose style and the enlarged perspective of his *History of Italy.*

Guicciardini's historical method was increasingly dependent upon original documentary evidence. One modern historian has suggested several reasons for Guicciardini's abandonment of *Florentine Affairs* for *The History of Italy.*[8] A primary explanation may have been that such a study of contemporary European affairs could more easily be based upon readily obtainable documents and records. Attempting to trace sources pertaining to Florentine history as far back as 1375 constituted a major problem in Guicciardini's day. Secondly, Guicciardini had already decided in 1528 to write a description of his own deeds while employed by the pope, and by 1535 he had already made numerous drafts of a work which treated events in Italy during 1525 and 1526. A nucleus for a new work of broader proportions, therefore, already existed. Finally, the death of Pope Clement in 1534 represented more than the end of Guicciardini's own political career. It also marked the end of Florence's political independence. A political history of the city no longer had the same importance as it had in Guicciardini's youth, since Florence was now only a satellite state within an area under Spanish domination. The struggle for power between unified European nation states was now the catalyst of events and the historical phenomenon important to any observant political analyst. The study of the city-state of Florence in *Florentine Affairs* no longer had any relevance in an age when such political entities were merely pawns in the larger European context, and Guicciardini's natural inclination was to turn to a subject more suitable to the political realities of his times and about which he could produce a history based upon accessible, verifiable, primary sources. It was Guicciardini's misfortune to be directed by his desire for precision and detail to a merciless dissection of the tragic decline of Italian greatness after a period of incomparable achievement.

CHAPTER 8

The History of Italy

*T*HE *History of Italy* displays a heavy reliance upon the humanist models, those practices constituting "the laws of history,"
as Guicciardini once called them.[1] Stylized battle scenes, paired
literary speeches, portents of impending disasters, and carefully
drawn literary portraits abound in the narrative. Guicciardini even
included in the papers comprising the manuscript of the work a
quotation from Cicero's *De Oratore* on the composition of true history:

The nature of the subject needs chronological arrangement and
geographical representation: . . . it calls also, as regards such plans, for some
imitation of what was done or said, but also of the manner of doing or saying
it; and, in the estimate of consequences, for an exposition of all contributory
causes, whether originating in accident, discretion or foolhardiness; and, as
for the individual actors, besides an account of their exploits, it demands
particulars of the lives and characters of such as are outstanding in renown
and dignity. Then again the kind of language and type of style to be
followed are the easy and the flowing, which run their course with un-
varying current and a certain placidity, avoiding alike the rough speech we
use in Court and the advocate's stinging epigrams.[2]

Cicero calls attention to several important traits of true history:
chronological arrangement, attention to detail (especially anecdotes
concerning the lives of the main characters), a search for historical
causes, and a pleasing, simple style. Guicciardini subscribes to this
prescription as much as possible, although he concurrently utilizes
his own innovative methods of research to prepare his historical account of Italian affairs between 1490 and 1534.

Guicciardini's *History of Italy* treats in great detail the events that
occurred in Italy during the period between 1490 and 1534. The title
referring to Italy is actually a misnomer, appended to the untitled

manuscript after the author's death, and the first line of the book reveals its broadly European scope: "I have determined to write about those events which have occurred in Italy within our memory, ever since French troops, summoned by our own princes, began to stir up very great dissensions here; a most memorable subject in view of its scope and variety, and full of the most terrible happenings."[3] It is the struggle for European hegemony between the various European states which occupies the historian's attention. Italian history is examined within the bounds of a broad, international perspective, and this viewpoint alone constitutes one of the work's conceptual innovations.

Begun around 1534 as a less comprehensive narrative of the events of 1525 and 1526, *The History of Italy* was thus to have concentrated, in a somewhat autobiographical manner, upon the years during which Guicciardini served the pope as Lieutenant-General in the League of Cognac. There exist no less than three manuscript versions of this "false start" which was later incorporated into the final work as Book Sixteen. After having revised this beginning several times, Guicciardini began dictating a different history to his secretary which returned to 1490 as its starting point. Several versions of the complete history in both Guicciardini's and the secretary's hands with autograph corrections have been preserved. Presently located in the Laurentian Library in Florence, the final copy was dictated in 1539 after the author suffered a serious attack of apoplexy. The last four books were completed without receiving a final revision, but the work stands as a whole and is not marred by the fragmentary character of the *Florentine Affairs*. Unlike Guicciardini's many other works which were never intended for publication, *The History of Italy* was written specifically for that purpose. Guicciardini even submitted the manuscript to a humanist friend, Giovanni Corsi, for his comments. Guicciardini accepted the suggestion to transform the narrative from nineteen to twenty books, since in Corsi's opinion the latter figure was "a more perfect number."[4] Guicciardini's death in 1540 prevented the work from appearing during his lifetime. In addition, Guicciardini reportedly requested on his deathbed that the manuscripts be burned.[5] Fortunately, his heirs were unwilling to fulfill this last wish. His wife retained his papers, passed them on to his brother Girolamo in 1543, and from 1545 until 1561, when the first printed edition appeared, the work was read in manuscript by a restricted audience of friends, humanists, and historians.

The revolutionary historical methods of *Florentine Affairs* are refined and expanded in *The History of Italy*. Guicciardini continued to make use of secondary works, especially other histories of Italian cities or wars. Practically every available work in both Latin or Italian pertaining to the period was considered either in printed form or in manuscript. Furthermore, Guicciardini relied to a much greater extent upon primary documents in *The History of Italy* than he had in his unfinished humanist narrative. Not only did he have his own private documents, letters, and memoirs which dealt with many of the most important events or personalities of the period, but he also obtained access to many official sources as well. The most striking instance of his research into such normally inaccessible state papers is his use of the entire archives of the Ten of War which he had carried to his private library in 1530. The Ten of War was the body in charge of Florentine military affairs and diplomacy, the equivalent of our Department of State, and its papers were an invaluable source of information on the international affairs of the epoch. Perhaps the most important distinction between *Florentine Affairs* and *The History of Italy* is that the author himself had lived through the events he describes in the latter work and was an important protagonist in many of them. Furthermore, because Guicciardini was acquainted personally with many of the popes, cardinals, princes, emperors, and kings who played crucial historical roles, his work comes alive with the veracity that only firsthand knowledge can provide.

I *The Birth of Philosophical History*

Were *The History of Italy* only a simple chronological narrative of political affairs during a normal period of Italian history, it would retain today little more than scholarly interest, and Francesco De Sanctis, surely no admirer of Guicciardini, would not have judged the work's intellectual power as constituting "the most important work that has ever issued from the Italian mind."[6] The work instead presents more than a collection of historical facts; it is a philosophical interpretation of human behavior during one of the most crucial periods in modern European history. It thus establishes a speculative tendency for future philosopher-historians like Voltaire, Gibbon, Montesquieu, Hegel, and Croce and appreciably broadens the vistas of the discipline of history. Central to Guicciardini's interpretation of events in Italy from 1490 until 1534 is his view, expressed earlier in *The History of Florence* without drawing out its implications, that the death of Lorenzo il Magnifico and the French invasion of Italy in 1494 constituted a turning point in modern European history and not just in the history of the Italian peninsula or the city of Florence. The first hint of the radical changes which were to transform Guicciardini's world were the technical innovations in warfare itself. The invention of artillery, "this diabolical rather than human weapon," changed the nature of warfare by making the almost impregnable medieval cities and their massive walls vulnerable to seige.[7] Instead of the customary battles of the past which had often been little more than military parades, the "barbarians" who invaded Italy brought with them a savagery and a thirst for blood which amazed the more civilized Italians. It was "a thing unheard of and very frightening in Italy, which for a long time had been used to seeing wars staged with beautiful pomp and display, not unlike spectacles, rather than waged with bloodshed and dangers."[8] The year 1494 spells the beginning of the end for the political independence of the city-states and small principalities of Italy and the gradual eclipse of Italy as the center of world affairs — "a most unhappy year for Italy, and in truth the beginning of those years of misfortune, because it opened the door to innumerable horrible calamities, in which, one could say, for various reasons, a great part of the world was subsequently involved."[9]

The view that these events initiated a great upheaval of the established order in the world eventually required that Guicciardini reinterpret his earlier view of Lorenzo de' Medici. In his *History of Florence*, Lorenzo had been criticized as a genial tyrant, but there Guicciardini clearly preferred a form of aristocratic government wherein many of the great families of the city would have divided the power held by the single Medici family. With the emergence of a new European community of sovereign states guided by a policy of expansionism and foreign conquest, Guicciardini radically modifies this earlier opinion, apparently feeling the preservation of Italian political independence at the price of Florentine liberty to be worth the sacrifice. Consequently, he views Lorenzo as the main stabilizing force in the political scene before 1494:

Many factors kept her in that state of felicity, which was the consequence of various causes. But it was most commonly agreed that, among these, no small praise should be attributed to the industry and skill of Lorenzo de' Medici, so eminent among the ordinary rank of citizens in the city of Florence that the affairs of that republic were governed according to his counsels. . . . Realizing that it would be most perilous to the Florentine Republic and to himself if any of the major powers should extend their area of domination, he carefully saw to it that the Italian situation should be maintained in a state of balance, not leaning more toward one side than the other.[10]

Guicciardini formulates here not only a view of Italian history that has been almost uncritically accepted for centuries, but also the basic concept of the "balance of power" which has ever since been applied to the analysis of European history and international affairs.

The picture Guicciardini draws of Italy before 1494 portrays an idyllic state of peace and prosperity. Not only was Italy politically independent and economically strong, but she also dazzled all of Europe with the magnificence of her cities, the pomp of her courts, the inventiveness of her artists, and the brilliance of her writers so that "she deservedly held a celebrated name and reputation among all the nations."[11] The contrast of this achievement and the upheavals which swept all aside by 1534 forms the nucleus of Guicciardini's history. From the vantage point of an observer who has survived the disaster, Guicciardini presents the contemporary history of the Italian peninsula as a great tragedy which unfolds in various stages.[12] The fall of Italy represented the end of an entire system of government and customs dear to Guicciardini. The eclipse of the city - state system, the quintessential expression of Italian Renaissance genius, also represented the passing away of the political ascendancy of Guicciardini's own social class. He leaves no doubts in our minds that the changes set in motion in 1494 were fundamental:

Charles entered Asti on the ninth day of September of the year 1494, bringing with him into Italy the seeds of innumerable calamities, of most horrible events and changes in almost the entire state of affairs. For his passage into Italy not only gave rise to changes of dominations, subversion of kingdoms, desolation of countries, destruction of cities and the cruelest massacres, but also new fashions, new customs, new and bloody ways of waging warfare, and diseases which had been unknown up to that time. Furthermore, his incursion introduced so much disorder into Italian ways of governing and maintaining harmony, that we have never since been able to re-establish order, thus opening the possibility to other foreign nations and barbarous armies to trample upon our institutions and miserably oppress us.[13]

The first two books introduce the entrance of Charles VIII into Italy and explain this invasion by describing the policies of Lodovico

Sforza of Milan and the Borgia Pope, Alexander VI. Guicciardini then probes their motives, goals and achievements. After their disappearance from the historical scene, the invasion they have brought about by their policies continues unchecked as subsequent French rulers (Louis XII, François I), Spanish monarchs (Charles V), and Italian princes are drawn deeper into a whirlpool of events over which no one apparently has any veritable control. After 1521, the Italians no longer initiate political events but simply suffer the effects of the conflicts of foreign powers on their own territory as Italy becomes Europe's battleground. Guicciardini's history ends after Spanish hegemony in Italy has been established. Florence and other formerly independent city-states become satellites of Charles V, and the position of Italy in the world is completely and irrevocably modified, almost as if its former greatness had been an illusion.

II *The Tragedy of Self-Interest*

The scope of the tragedy which befell Italy demanded an explanation from Guicciardini. It seemed to many of his contemporaries that Italy's endless problems were the result of a divine wrath, and Guicciardini mentions that divine punishment is one possibility: "for so many years Italy suffered all those calamities with which miserable mortals are usually afflicted, sometimes because of the just anger of God, and sometimes because of the impiety and wickedness of other men."[14] Transcendental explanations in Guicciardini's narrative are, however, rarely advanced seriously as historical causes. The "impiety and wickedness" of the historical characters he studies provide sufficient material to suggest an explanation for various disasters. In other works, Guicciardini had advanced the theory that human nature was intrinsically good but weak and easily corruptible by self-interest. This *particulare* in man constitutes the source of his destructive greed, ambition, and short-sightedness. Guicciardini's analysis of the actions of the great princes and pontiffs of the day reveals a state of affairs in which the element of self-interest runs amuck on an international scale. Rulers and the nations they govern are corrupted by their narrowly defined regional interests. Consequently, Italian states destroy themselves in their schemes to use foreign arms to rid themselves of other Italian opponents. Even against the Turks, a common political and religious enemy, unity proves impossible: "since each of them considered the danger uncertain and very far off, and relating more to one state than to another, and since it was very difficult, and required a long time to introduce such a sense of zeal and so universal a union, private interests and advantages prevailed."[15]

This statement summarizes succinctly part of Guicciardini's explanation of Italy's fall. As any good humanist historian might, Guicciardini notes in the opening lines of the work that "from a knowledge of such occurrences, so varied and so grave, everyone may derive many precedents salutary both for himself and for the public weal."[16] Positive *exempla* in the work, however, are conspicuously absent. The political lessons imparted by Guicciardini's work are almost all negative ones, descriptions of actions to be avoided rather than to be imitated. Man's basic characteristic is defined as ambition, but it is not often the beneficial spirit of ambition delineated in the *Ricordi*, the ambition that spurs noble men on to great deeds that honor not only their name and lineage but also their city or nation. The quality of ambition Guicciardini now sees operative in Italian history is a blind, selfish, morally unredemptive force resulting in both personal and civic disaster. Even the victors are not spared from this judgment. Charles VIII, King of France, entered Italy as a conqueror, overturned governments that seemed immutable, and on his return to France dealt an Italian army a disgraceful defeat at the battle of Fornovo. But such a man was far from an admirable figure; he was a moral monster:

and what is all the more disgraceful, we cannot mitigate our shame because of the valor of the victor, since he whose coming caused so many misfortunes was, although well endowed in wealth and fortune, almost completely devoid of any natural or mental gifts. . . . Indeed, if anything in him seemed worthy of praise, if one looked at it more closely, it proved to be further from virtue than from vice.[17]

Other leaders fared no better under Guicciardini's scrutiny. Pope Julius II, unjustly better known for his stormy relationship with Michelangelo than for his many achievements as a prince of the church, was judged to be of "inestimable spirit and resolution, but impetuous and given to boundless schemes, and if these traits did not hurl him to his ruin, he was sustained more by the feeling of reverence felt toward the Church, the disagreement among princes and the conditions of the times, than by moderation and

prudence."[18] Guicciardini shows King Louis XII of France to have
destroyed himself by excessive lovemaking, crowning a lifetime of
political failures with personal debauchery.

III   *The Borgia Legend*

The most despicable of all the characters in Guicciardini's rogues'
gallery are the Borgias. Even in a history as accurate as Guicciardini's, the description of their nefarious activities, which have
become legendary, are often based more upon myth or hearsay than
reality. In Book Three, Guicciardini relates how not only Pope Alexander VI but also his sons Cesare, the Duke of Valentinois, and
Giovanni, the Duke of Gandia, competed for the incestuous favors of
his daughter and their sister Lucrezia:

It was equally rumored (if however it is possible to believe so great an enor-
mity) that not only the two brothers, but the father himself, competed for
the love of Madonna Lucrezia; since, as soon as he was made pontiff, he had
separated her from her first husband as having become inferior to her rank,
and married her off to Giovanni Sforza, lord of Pesaro. But not being able to
tolerate having even her husband as a rival, he dissolved this matrimony
which had already been consummated; having proved with false witnesses
before judges which he had chosen, and later confirmed by a sentence, that
Giovanni was frigid by nature and impotent in coitus.[19]

The pope himself is pictured as a man so obsessed by a lust for
power, monetary gain, and sensual satisfaction that he is oblivious to
the threats confronting the temporal power of the Papacy: "Nor had
the Pope taken any provisions against such disorders in the
Ecclesiastical State because he hated to spend money on such
things, and because his nature was little disturbed by the calamity of
others so that he was not at all troubled by those things which
offended his honor, provided that his profits and pleasures were in
no way impeded."[20]

Guicciardini also reports the story, widely believed at the time,
that Pope Alexander and Cesare Borgia attempted to murder the
Cardinal of Corneto with poisoned wine but only succeeded in
drinking the potion themselves because of a steward's error, bringing about the death of the pope and the sickness and ultimate
political ruin of his warrior son. Guicciardini had labeled the story
about Lucrezia a rumor, and it is to his credit that he again com-

ments that his explanation of the pope's death was that described in the "most widespread rumor" of the day, even though everyone "believed that this episode was the result of poison."[21] In spite of this admirable reluctance on the part of one of the most careful of all Renaissance historians to give credence to what was essentially a result of spiteful gossip, Guicciardini nevertheless believed, as did his contemporaries, that the Borgias habitually managed their affairs with the assistance of deadly poisons administered in as deceitful a manner as possible: "it is clear that both father and son had frequently and habitually made use of poison, not only to take revenge against their enemies and secure themselves against suspicions, but also because of their wicked greed to despoil the wealthy of their possessions, both amongst the cardinals and other members of the court, heedless of the fact that they had never been harmed in any way by these people."[22] If there was any question in the historian's mind about the veracity of these rumors he reports in his narrative, the picture he shows of the reaction of the Roman populace to the pope's death leaves no question about what Guicciardini thought of the man himself: "All Rome thronged with incredible rejoicing to see the dead body of Alexander in Saint Peter's, unable to satiate their eyes enough with seeing spent that serpent who in his boundless ambition and pestiferous perfidy, and with all his examples of horrible cruelty and monstrous sensuality and unheard-of avarice, selling without distinction sacred and profane things, had envenomed the entire world."[23] Guicciardini submits that the life of this prince of the church is an excellent proof that the argument that "the prosperity or adversity of men proceeds from their own merits or demerits" has no basis in fact, and he calls this biography "a powerful example to confound the arrogance of those who, presuming to discern with the weakness of human eyes the depth of divine judgments," attempt to read such meanings into the success or failure of various individuals.[24]

Modern historical research has shown that such accusations against the Borgia family were founded less upon any factual basis than upon cold political calculations on the part of the accusers.[25] Although the Borgias were no saints, almost none of the most serious rumors about them reported by Guicciardini, except perhaps their skill at simony, are true. And even the practice of simony was not unusual for the period. Much of the resentment against the Borgias can probably be traced both to their Spanish origin and to their relative success in using the Papacy for their own personal advantage, a talent secretly admired if publicly resented by many of the aspirants to St. Peter's throne. The popular picture that much of the English-speaking world has of the Italian Renaissance is often colored by an anti-Catholic, Protestant bias. It has sometimes seemed convenient for Protestants to believe that Italy was inhabited by poisoners, corrupt popes, and crafty statesmen who would achieve by murder and stealth that which was impossible by honest dealings. Without the myth of the "Machiavellian" villain or the picture Guicciardini paints of the corruption in the church, much of the flavor of English drama of the sixteenth and seventeenth centuries would be lost, since so much of it is set not in England but in the Italian peninsula. No amount of scholarly argument can undo, however, four centuries of popular error, and no doubt the common conception of Pope Alexander, Cesare and Lucrezia Borgia as murderers, tyrants, and libertines will continue forever. The fact that people who have never read a page of any Renaissance history vaguely know this evil legend is a testament to the impact of Guicciardini's *History of Italy* upon the Western imagination, albeit an impression which the careful historian would have been the first to disavow in the face of the evidence marshalled by recent historians.

IV *Critique of Papal Power*

Guicciardini enlarges his critique of individual pontiffs to make a broader attack upon the secular power of the church in general. In Book Four, he emphasizes the falsity of the Donation of Constantine which had been used for centuries by the church as a basis for its argument that temporal rulers are subject to papal authority. The most important work proving the document a forgery by the sound philological methods of textual analysis devised by the Italian humanist movement was the *De falso credita et ementita Constantini donatione declamatio* of Lorenzo Valla (1405 - 1457) which had appeared in 1440. Guicciardini, not one to read theological works for enjoyment, no doubt examined this document for its political and not its philological importance. Guicciardini declares that much of the demand for ecclesiastical reform is provoked not by heresy but by the obvious corruption of the church's spiritual mission. Although he personally rejects Lutheran ideas as "pestiferous poison," Guicciardini indignantly criticizes in Book Thirteen the scandalous selling of indulgences practiced by his own patron, Pope Leo X:

Since there was no precedent or truth of any sort in this procedure, for it was notorious that these indulgences were being granted only to extort money from men who yielded more out of simplicity than out of wisdom, and since the practice was being impudently carried on by commissioners deputized for these exactions, most of whom purchased the right of selling indulgences at the court, they had stirred up a great deal of scandal and indignation in many places; and especially in Germany where many of the Pope's ministers were seen selling at a cheap price, or gambling away in the taverns, the power of delivering the souls of the dead out of Purgatory.[26]

Furthermore, in Book Ten he includes an antipapal speech by Pompeo Colonna, Bishop of Rieti, which compares the pontiffs to oriental despots in their practices:

In the entire world there are two similar principalities: the Roman pontiffs and the sultans of Cairo. For neither the dignity of the sultanate nor the highest offices of the Mamelukes are hereditary, but passing from person to person, are granted even to foreigners; and nevertheless the servitude of the Romans is even more ignominious than that of the peoples of Egypt and Syria; insofar as the ignominy of the latter is to some degree understandable because of the bellicose, ferocious nature of the Mamelukes, men inured to toils and lives without any softness or delicacy. But whom are the Romans serving? Persons who are slothful and indolent; foreigners, and often most ignoble not only by blood but also by their mode of behavior.[27]

Guicciardini's position, it should be noted, was anticlerical, not antireligious. Nevertheless, for many years to come, Counter-Reformation censors would suspect several passages in his history of containing possible heretical statements. In one of these, Guicciardini relates his observation on the discovery of America and its implications for the omniscient character of the Holy Scriptures:

These voyages have not only confuted many things which had been affirmed by writers about terrestrial matters, but besides this, they have given some cause for alarm to interpreters of the Holy Scriptures, who are accustomed to interpret those verses of the Psalms in which it is declared that the sound of their songs had gone over all the earth and their words spread to the edges of the world, as meaning that faith in Christ had spread over the entire earth through the mouths of the Apostles: an interpretation contrary to the truth, because since no knowledge of these lands had hitherto been brought to light, nor have any signs or relics of our faith been found there, it is unworthy to be believed, either that faith in Christ had existed there before these times, or that so vast a part of the world had never before been discovered or found by men of our hemisphere.[28]

Elsewhere, another description of an election within the College of Cardinals rather cynically dismisses the idea that divine inspiration could have had anything to do with the choice of a pope: "as if the Holy Ghost, which above all loves the purest hearts and spirits, would not disdain to enter into souls full of ambition and incredible greed, and almost all dedicated to the most refined, not to say most dishonest, pleasures."[29] Neither of these passages, expurgated from all Italian editions of *The History of Italy* until the eighteenth century, shock us today, but they do reveal that Guicciardini's constant approach to history is an unrelentingly honest one. Caring little for the sophisticated theological disputes of the day, Guicciardini's reaction to church corruption was that of a simple and devout Christian. His reaction as a historian and political analyst was another matter, for, like Machiavelli, he concentrates only upon the institutional aspects of the church and not upon its admittedly important but tangential spiritual values in his works. Nevertheless, in spite of Guicciardini's orthodox religious beliefs, his revelations of corruption and decadence within the church hierarchy are sufficient to justify several reformations, and much of the work's popularity abroad in years to come would be based on its usefulness as a source for Protestant propaganda.

V *The Medici Popes: Historical Portraiture*

Something was rotten in Guicciardini's Italy, and as in *Hamlet*, the decay began at the top. More than any previous modern history, Guicciardini's *History of Italy* establishes a close causal connection between history and human psychology. Because of the importance of the personalities of historical figures in explaining the causal links between historical events, Guicciardini often inserts portraits or character sketches in his narrative in order to provide concrete examples of political decisions to emulate or to avoid. Many are masterpieces of expository prose, brilliant epigrammatic insights into the innermost secrets of a prince, pope, or king. Perhaps the most interesting of these is the comparison of the two Medici prelates — Leo X and Clement VII. Another contemporary historian, Francesco Vettori, had compared the two pontiffs in his *Summary of Italian History from 1511 to 1527*.[30] Vettori had concluded that Leo X committed error after error, but he was always blessed with fortune's favor and emerged from his errors unscathed. In contrast, Vettori believed that Clement VII attempted to avoid danger and to rule prudently, but his every project came to a disastrous conclusion, as in the sack of Rome, because of fortune's decree. Vettori thus interpreted the actions of each man in the light of the impact of an omnipotent *fortuna* or chance upon human affairs.

Like Vettori, Guicciardini appreciates the role of chance in historical affairs, but his analysis of the two popes is more subtle in its psychological realism. Recalling Vettori, Guicciardini pictures Leo as profligate, and overly devoted to fleshly pleasures (especially "those pleasures which cannot honestly be mentioned"), although he is indeed most fortunate in all his schemes. Most of the observers at the Roman court attributed Leo's success not only to *fortuna* but also to his reliance upon the then cardinal Giulio de' Medici. Thus,

the assiduousness, the diligence, the order, the gravity of habits of the one; the easygoingness, the prodigality, the pleasures and sense of honor of the other, made many people think that Leo was ruled by Giulio, and that in himself he was not the man to hold so heavy a responsibility, nor to do harm to anyone, but simply most desirous to enjoy the comforts of the pontificate; and on the contrary, that Giulio was ambitious, thirsting for innovations, with the result that all the severity, all the agitation, all the enterprises that took place during the time of Leo, were believed to have proceeded at Giulio's instigation, who was reputed to be a malevolent man, but of great mind and capacity.[31]

Guicciardini finds the most convincing explanation for the diverse fortunes of these two men in their individual personalities and not simply in the operation of blind chance alone. It is Leo's nature that insures his often unmerited successes, for he possesses the quality of resolution and decisiveness which Giulio lacks. Even though all had believed upon Giulio's election that he would be "a greater pope and accomplish greater deeds than any of those who till that day had been seated in that chair," it soon became clear that popular opinion had erred:

For Giulio had many characteristics different from those which had previously been believed: he did not possess either that desire for change, or grandeur, or tendency of mind for generous and magnanimous ends that had been previously supposed, and had been rather Leo's executor and minister of his plans far more than the director and initiator of his counsels and of his will. And although he had a most capable intelligence and marvelous knowledge of world affairs, yet he lacked the corresponding resolution and execution . . . so that he remained almost always in suspension and ambiguous when he was faced with deciding those things which from afar he had many times foreseen, considered, and almost resolved. Whence, both in his deliberations and in executing what he had already decided upon, any small aspect newly revealing itself, any slight impediment that might cross his path, seemed sufficient to make him fall back into that confusion wherein he was before he had come to a decision, since it always seemed to him, once he had decided, that the counsel which he had rejected was better. For afterward, summoning up in his mind only those reasons which he had neglected, he did not recall those reasons which had motivated his choice.[32]

Like Machiavelli, Guicciardini rejects timid behavior when the times call for bold and decisive action in the face of crisis. Guicciardini's intimate portrait of Clement VII, a man whom he knew personally and for whom he labored for so long in vain, is a masterpiece of psychological introspection. In only a few sentences, Guicciardini has captured the soul of a very complicated individual and has explained how his character shaped and defined much of his political behavior. Although human history may frequently be the plaything of *fortuna* in *The History of Italy*, human weaknesses and personal character traits are often the immediate source of *fortuna*'s effects upon the course of events, the "raw material" molded by the power of chance or fate.

The illusions, fear, ambitions, and errors of men are now an integral part of the mechanism of human affairs which are shown by Guicciardini to follow only very infrequently a rational pattern or a predictable trajectory. The faith in history as a source of imitable political lessons that burned so strongly in Machiavelli's works is completely absent. A study of Guicciardini's historical characters helps to illuminate the causal connections between apparently unrelated events. Such analyses may reveal why developments occurred as they did, but they have little power to predict the future course of events. Guicciardini had made this attack upon Machiavelli and the humanist tradition very plain in the *Ricordi*. He now supplements his theory with a perfect historical example to illustrate why patterning one's actions after past events is almost impossible. In 1494, Piero de' Medici found himself in a very difficult position, having attempted to oppose the French invasion of Charles VIII in the face of strong pro-French sentiment within the city. He thus succeeded in alienating both his major foreign ally and his domestic supporters, bringing upon himself a French invasion. Piero remembered the action of his father Lorenzo il Magnifico in 1479 who, when reduced to almost certain defeat in a war waged against

Pope Sixtus and King Ferdinand of Naples, went personally to
parley with the Neapolitans. Through the force of his own courage,
Lorenzo thus established a peace that reigned in Italy until his
death. When Piero tried to repeat this feat by a visit to the French
king's camp, he succeeded only in losing complete control of
Florence, as a revolution established a republic in Florence during
his absence. Guicciardini concludes that "governing oneself by examples is undoubtedly very dangerous if similar circumstances do
not correspond, not only in general but in all particulars, and if
things are not managed with similar judgment, and if, aside from all
other fundamentals, one does not have similar good fortune on one's
side."[33] This statement partially duplicates the content of maxim C-
117, but it is even more critical than the earlier opinion in its attack
upon the central tenet of humanist historiography, the doctrine of
imitation, because it adds the additional caveat that exact duplica-
tion of events will not produce the same results without the element
of chance or luck. It is a pessimistic picture indeed, without any
glimmer of hope for the reader who would have been accustomed to
read history in order to learn from the past and to avoid the mistakes
of others. For, if man cannot learn to improve his behavior by im-
itating exemplary deeds of the past, he cannot hope to learn how to
avoid those events in the past which do not coincide with his goals.

VI   Fortuna *in Human Affairs*

In Guicciardini's history, the pagan goddess *Fortuna* is revived
and assumes a key role in historical explanations. As long as Italians
could view the invasion of their territory as a temporary in-
convenience, the blame could still be placed upon the shoulders of a
few irresponsible princes or could be attributed to the justifiable
anger of a wrathful God. As it became clearer that the French invasion was part of a larger European struggle for power in which the
Italians were no longer participants but increasingly simple victims
or pawns, the event began to be viewed more seriously as a result of
some superhuman power beyond comprehension. *Fortuna* or chance
became increasingly popular as an explanation in the historical and
political literature of the period. As Felix Gilbert puts it, "whereas in
the earlier times *Fortuna's* influence was limited to special spheres
or definite occasions, the *Fortuna* which emerged as the ruler of
world history in the sixteenth century was the power behind
everything that happened: it was an embodiment of the uncon-
trollable forces determining the course of events."[34]

The change in philosophical attitude from a more optimistic interpretation of the role of chance in human affairs to this pessimistic,
fatalistic vision of Italian history is best exemplified by the divergent
viewpoints of Guicciardini and Machiavelli. For Machiavelli, *fortuna* was an important element to be included in all political
calculations, but man was not completely dominated by this blind
force. In *The Prince*, Machiavelli devotes an entire chapter to this
problem. He agrees only partially with those who, like Guicciardini,
would maintain that chance controls most of human activity. Argu-
ing strongly for free will, Machiavelli says:

> I think it may be true that fortune is the ruler of half our actions, but that she
> allows the other half or thereabouts to be governed by us. I would compare
> her to an impetuous river that, when turbulent, inundates the plains, casts
> down trees and buildings, removes earth from this side and places it on the
> other; every one flees before it, and everything yields to its fury without be-
> ing able to oppose it; and yet though it is of such a kind, still when it is quiet,
> men can make provision against it by dykes and banks, so that when it rises
> it will either go into a canal or its rush will not be so wild and dangerous.[35]

In Machiavelli's opinion, Italy is a state without the necessary dams
or banks to prevent the floods of *fortuna*. His new prince will
remedy such a situation. Far from the misanthropic, pessimistic attitude most criticism usually attributes to Machiavelli, his ideas op-
timistically assert man's capacity to shape his own destiny. For
Machiavelli, it is the bold and virtuous prince whose decisive actions
will bend *fortuna* to his own will:

> I certainly think it is better to be impetuous than cautious, for fortune is a
> woman, and it is necessary, it you wish to master her, to conquer her by
> force; and it can be seen that she lets herself be overcome by the bold rather
> than by those who proceed coldly. And therefore, like a woman, she is
> always a friend to the young, because they are less cautious, fiercer, and
> master her with greater audacity.[36]

Machiavelli's approach to such philosophical problems is here, as
always, more poetic and intuitional than analytic. With his striking
metaphors and images, he sweeps away any objections or qualifications.

Guicciardini, however, is the master of the qualification, the
lingering doubt, the embarrassing question which yields to no quick

answer or poetic image. He seldom allows himself to be carried away from his relentless dissection of the tragedy of Italy by poetic flights of the imagination, although in one instance, he uses a telling metaphor to describe historical events, which he views as so changeable that they are "not unlike a sea whipped by winds."[37] For Guicciardini, a practical acquaintance with politics reveals how seemingly unimportant occurrences can be used by *fortuna* to destroy even the best organized plans. *The History of Italy* is therefore filled with vignettes that illustrate this view. It is important not to overlook the moralistic, didactic element of this work which is commonly described as the first "modern," and therefore nonmoralistic, history of Europe. A favorite theme of medieval moralists and fifteenth-century humanists was that of the fall of princes or time's revenge, and events demonstrating these subjects abound in the pages of Guicciardini's narrative.[38] The most striking scene of this type describes the fall of Lodovico Sforza, Duke of Milan, after his capture by the King of France:

thus within a narrow prison were enclosed the thoughts and ambitions of one whose ideas earlier could scarcely be contained within the limits of all Italy — a prince certainly most excellent in eloquence, in skill and many other qualities of mind and nature, and worthy of obtaining a name . . . so varied and miserable is human destiny and so uncertain to everyone are his own conditions in times to come.[39]

The battle of Fornovo provides Guicciardini with an opportunity to expose the vast unpredictability of history:

But (as everyone knows) the power of fortune is most great in all human affairs, ever more in military matters than any others, but inestimable, immense and infinite in actual warfare; where a badly understood command, or a poorly executed order, or an act of rashness, or a false rumor, sometimes coming from even the simplest soldier, will often bring victory to those who already seem to be defeated, and where innumerable accidents unexpectedly occur which cannot be foreseen or controlled by the captain's orders.[40]

The arbitrary force of fortune even disrupts the progressive successes of Giovanni de' Medici who, as the papal legate of Julius II, is captured by the French after the disastrous battle of Ravenna. Despite this debacle, he is elected to the papacy as Leo X shortly thereafter; "and what made this day all the more memorable and all the more extraordinary was the realization that he who now was accepting, with such unusual pomp and splendor, the banners of so many high dignitaries, had been on the very same day, a year before, taken prisoner."[41] Guicciardini could never resist the temptation to point out the irrationality present in human affairs. The last description of the history, a passage treating the ascension of Paul III to the papacy on the death of Clement VII, links Paul's good fortune with the beauty of a woman. Pope Alexander Borgia had elevated him to the College of Cardinals years earlier not because of his personal merits but because of the charms of his sister. Thus, a passing affair, and not the divine inspiration commonly assumed to be operative in such matters, is ultimately responsible for the election of a pope to the office of St. Peter.

Unlike humanist historians who had justified the study of history on the basis of its didactic lessons, Guicciardini repeatedly questions such a practical use of history, not only because he doubts the validity of the historical *exemplum* but also because of the almost omnipotent power of *fortuna* which rules history without following any discernible pattern or purpose. By implication, human reason is severely limited. Rarely, Guicciardini shows, does success result from following the dictates of reason. In discussing the need for rulers to seek advice from their counselors, Guicciardini reveals how deceptive are the claims of those who, like Machiavelli, would offer rules for princes to follow. Certainly nothing is more necessary in deliberations, Guicciardini admits, and nothing is, on the other hand, more dangerous than to ask advice. No ruler's judgment is so perfect that he can afford to ignore wise counsel from his courtiers. Yet, the problem is to obtain advice untainted by self-interest, and a courtier offers only advice "toward that end which turns more to his advantage or is more suitable for his purposes; and since these ends are usually unknown to the person seeking advice, he is not aware, unless he is wise, of the faithlessness of the counsel." [42] There seems to be no solution to the dilemma because there is so little possibility of transcending the egoism inherent in human nature. Machiavelli consistently declares that man is naturally selfish and evil, yet paradoxically he also holds out the possibility that Renaissance Italians may transcend this inherent human condition with a titanic effort to reestablish ancient *virtù* under the dynamic rule of a new prince, ridding Italy of the foreign "barbarians" in the process. The self-sacrifice and heroism envisioned by Machiavelli's theories are reduced in Guicciardini to a hedonistic calculus of petty human ambitions, desires, and fears. Nonetheless, the critics of the Italian

Risorgimento incorrectly assumed that Guicciardini gives sanction to this state of affairs. He believes that his pessimistic conclusions are simply empirical observations based upon events he had witnessed during his lifetime.

This bleak assessment of human capabilities is made no brighter by the faint hope of divine intervention or a grand plan in the historical process. The siege of Rome and the desecration of its temples, convents, and monasteries provoke Guicciardini's assertion that "God's judgments were beclouded and concealed from mortal men."[43] The payment of ransom raised through the sale of church property by Clement VII to rid himself of the Protestant mercenary soldiers after the siege moves Guicciardini to exclaim that "thus those things dedicated to the cult of God were, by concession of the Vicar of Christ, put to the use and maintenance of heretics (so unfathomable is divine justice)."[44] History offers, therefore, no teleological goal to be revealed to the human spirit nor any material to be shaped by human plan.

What purpose, then, did history finally fulfill for Guicciardini? If it could not teach the reader specific patterns of conduct to follow or to avoid, history could nevertheless impart a philosophical attitude, a point of view from which to contemplate the follies of human nature. As Felix Gilbert has put it, "although Guicciardini did not share the humanist view that history exemplifies general rules or guides man's behavior, he returned to the humanist concept of the moral value of history; history appeals to man to become conscious of his own intrinsic value."[45] *The History of Italy* is a depiction of human nature in action, presented in a mercilessly realistic manner, yet set within a vividly dazzling panorama of events and personalities that cannot fail to hold the reader's attention. Guicciardini's subject, like Montaigne's in his *Essais*, finally becomes simply man himself. History, rather than being regarded as a means to another end, that of predicting the future course of events or of guiding political action, becomes an end in itself. Its object of study, the human condition, assumes a philosophical importance in Guicciardini's work which his rejection of historiography's practical, didactic purposes could not obscure.

CHAPTER 9

Guicciardini and World Literature: An Assessment

THE story of Francesco Guicciardini's reputation reveals something of the reception accorded his works while it reflects general intellectual trends in Western culture. Like those of the even more famous Machiavelli, Guicciardini's fortunes both in his own country and abroad were often influenced more by extraliterary factors than by a sober, reasoned assessment of the merits of his political and historical writings. Because of the peculiar publication history of the works, a comprehensive view of Guicciardini's writings, their development, and their significance was perhaps not even possible until this century.

Studying the translations of an author's works may be a valuable means of assessing his influence abroad and his importance in world literature. In Guicciardini's case, such a study shows how the changing tastes of educated readers have affected his popularity.[1] The first important discovery, one which arises from even a cursory examination of the many translations and editions of Guicciardini's works, discloses that his reputation was based upon a small but important portion of his complete works. It is equally significant that the work many contemporary critics consider Guicciardini's most important contribution, the *Ricordi*, was much less influential than *The History of Italy*. Since only *The History of Italy* was ever intended for publication by its author, the circulation and publication of the *Ricordi* was accidental. First printed in Paris (1576) and in Venice (1582) in unauthorized Italian editions based upon a version of Manuscript A (not the corrected and final version completed by Guicciardini in 1530), these maxims had a rather irregular history.

I Versions of the Ricordi Abroad

Editions based upon one or the other of these pirated versions were translated into Latin, French, Dutch, Spanish, and finally

English. Throughout the history of these translations, however, the translators or editors were apt to mix Guicciardini's maxims with their own or with those found in classical or contemporary sources well known to most educated writers. Jacopo Corbinelli's edition was put into French immediately during the same year it appeared in Paris in Italian (1576). To the 158 *ricordi* by Guicciardini, the translator added forty-two others from various classical works.[2] The collection was reprinted again in 1587, but thereafter attracted little notice. The Venetian edition of Fra Sisto, however, successfully sparked a great measure of interest in the political maxim in general. It was reprinted with a commentary by Remigio Fiorentino as *Propositioni overo Considerationi in materia di cose di Stato* (1583). This collection, edited by Francesco Sansovino, consisted of the maxims of Guicciardini and Remigio Fiorentino, Sansovino's own *Concetti politici* and the *Avvedimenti civili* of Gian Francesco Lottini.[3] Sansovino's edition achieved a measure of popular success and was reprinted in 1588, 1598, and 1608. One of Guicciardini's nephews, Lodovico (1521 - 1589), published a collection entitled *I Precetti et Sententie più notabili in materia di Stato di M. Francesco Guicciardini* in 1585 which was translated into Latin two years later. Furthermore, incomplete translations of Fra Sisto's Venetian edition were made both in France by Gabriele Chappuys and in England by an Englishman known to us only by the initials "W. T."

The English version, appearing in 1601, was entitled *Civill Considerations upon Many and Sundrie Histories, as Well Ancient as Modern, and Principalie upon Those of Guicciardin*.[4] In spite of its title, this version followed the French version by Chappuys and contained only the commentary by Remigio Fiorentino. The English translator had completely disregarded the maxims by Guicciardini which were printed in the original edition. The Latin translation based upon Fra Sisto's original was actually more faithful and achieved a large circulation under the title *Hypomneses politicae* (1589); it was reprinted in 1598, 1599, 1600, 1601, 1609, 1610, and 1621.[5] Of more pertinence for the English-speaking public is an edition by Emma Martin in 1845 with parallel passages from Guicciardini, Machiavelli, Francis Bacon, Pascal, Montesquieu, and others.[6]

The appearance of so many versions of these maxims testifies to the currency of the philosophical and political aphorism during the Renaissance; but the rather cavalier manner in which Guicciardini's authorship was handled by some of the editors implies that their interest lay primarily in the subject matter and not in the author himself. Collections of aphorisms, sententious remarks, and general observations on politics or on "reason of state" were very much in vogue during the period. In fact, many editions of sententious remarks taken from Guicciardini's *History of Italy* were published separately or as appendages to the larger work, reflecting the reading public's predilection for such practical adages. Two English editions of the collection translated and edited by Sir Robert Dallington, *Aphorismes Civill and Militarie amplified with authorities and exemplified with Historie, out of the first Quarterne of Francis Guicciardinie*, appeared in London in 1613 and 1629.[7] Still, despite these various translations and adaptations of Guicciardini's *Ricordi*, this work remained largely unknown and was considered relatively unimportant by scholars until Giuseppe Canestrini published the maxims of both autograph manuscripts found in the Guicciardini family archives in 1857. Since that time, the work has increasingly attracted the attention of historians, political theorists, and Renaissance specialists and has received two excellent English translations in the last few years.[8] The consensus of opinion presently ranks the *Ricordi* alongside Guicciardini's *History of Italy* in intrinsic importance, even if its influence during the period of the Renaissance was slighter. In fact, the revival of interest in Guicciardini during the last century after the publication of the Canestrini edition has with some frequency centered around a debate over the significance of the *Ricordi*.

II *European Dimensions of* The History of Italy

It is to an analysis of the translations of Guicciardini's most important historical work that we must turn if we are to be able to assess the major impact of this writer upon world literature until the nineteenth century. And here there is a wealth of information to indicate that Guicciardini was one of the most widely read historians of the modern period, particularly during the Renaissance, the Reformation, and the Enlightenment. Translations of *The History of Italy* were not only more numerous than those of the *Ricordi*, but they were also more influential, having been translated by men who were able to disseminate Guicciardini's ideas on a broader scale. After the publication of the Florentine *editio princeps* in 1561, editions of the work appeared with great regularity during the sixteenth century. The first Latin version appeared in 1566 and was reprinted in 1567. It was the work of an Italian Protestant exile, Celio Secondo Curione (1503 - 1569) and was published in Basel,

Switzerland, a center of Protestant publication and propaganda.[9]
Many foreigners came to know of this work through the Latin edition, for it must not be forgotten that Latin, as well as Italian,
remained the universal language of intellectuals in Europe until
French began to displace it in the seventeenth century. Curione's
translation omitted the passages censored in the 1561 edition by
Bartolomeo Concini, the secretary of Cosimo I, Grand Duke of
Tuscany, since Curione had no reason to believe that the 1561 edition was incomplete when he made his translation.[10] Other Protestant writers and translators would not miss an opportunity to popularize historical observations or anecdotes so potentially damaging
to the Catholic cause when the expurgated passages later became
available from manuscripts of the complete work which had
remained in circulation even after the publication of the expurgated
1561 edition. In question were portions of several books: the
description of the incestuous relationships of the Borgia family in
Book Three; the explanation of the origin and progress of the
papacy's temporal power in Book Four; the remarks about the
effects the discovery of America might have upon the validity of the
Holy Scriptures; and the critique of papal political power in Rome in
Book Ten. While Protestants might accept some of this material
without question in order to damage the reputation of the Catholic
Church and to substantiate their claims that a reformation was
necessary, Catholics could also see in these passages traces of heresy
and grounds for placing the work on the Index. Thus, Guicciardini
inadvertently composed a work destined to become part of a
polemical debate over the causes of the Protestant Reformation.

Because of the close commercial, artistic, and intellectual ties
between Florence and France, it was only natural that one of the
most influential translations of the history abroad would be in
French. Only five years after the first Florentine edition in Italian,[11]
Hierôme de Chomedey published a translation which was dedicated
to Catherine de' Medici, Regent of France.[12] The translation had
been made from one of the numerous manuscripts in circulation and
not from the original Italian, since it contained some of the passages
deleted from the 1561 version. Thus, this translation is of special importance, since it was the first edition in any language to publish the
rumors of the Borgia incests. Such a scandalous revelation, in both
Protestant and Catholic circles, did much to insure Guicciardini an
avid audience in an age which seized upon any spicy rumor as a
weapon against its religious opponents.

It is also a matter of interest that the Italian printer who had published Curione's Latin translation was Pietro Perna (1520-1582), another Italian Protestant exile in Basel. Perna also published an important little book in 1569 in Latin, Italian, and French containing the two controversial passages from Books Three and Four on the Borgias and on the origins of the temporal power of the papacy.[13] This edition initiated a long series of separate printings of the controversial passages from the history which were manipulated by Protestants for anti-Catholic propaganda. It is a measure of Perna's estimation of Guicciardini's history as a Protestant source book that the first German translation by George Forberger was published by him in 1574, based upon Curione's Latin translation as well as upon an acquaintance with the original, complete Italian edition.

Chomedey's French translation was extremely popular during the period and was reprinted under his name twice in 1577, and again in 1593, 1612, and 1632. Subsequent editions of 1738 and 1836 failed to indicate that they were actually reprintings of his translation. The first Dutch translation of 1599 was based upon Chomedey and not upon an Italian original. More important, however, for Guicciardini's reception abroad was the use of the French translation to prepare the first English version of the history. This highly valued translation was published in 1579 by Geoffrey Fenton and was dedicated to Queen Elizabeth. Unfaithful to the original beyond his initial reliance upon a French translation, Fenton sometimes elaborates upon anti-French passages and underlines, as a Protestant apologist, material which might support this cause. Fenton was an important link between English and Italian culture during the early Renaissance even though he knew no Italian. In addition to his version of Guicciardini, he produced an English version of thirteen *novelle* by Bandello from a French translation which had already appeared in 1567 as *Certeine tragicall discourses*.[14]

Fenton's edition was republished in 1599 and 1618, and it included the section from Book Three on the incestuous affairs of the Borgias. The first edition omits, however, passages from Books Four and Ten on the temporal power of the papacy, but the third edition adds the section from Book Four. This particular passage, incidentally, was reprinted in English as a separate publication in 1706, 1712, 1729, 1827, 1853, and 1860, proof that even in eras of reduced religious strife, Protestant England maintained an interest in anti-Catholic propaganda. A second, almost complete translation by another hand was done in the eighteenth century by an Englishman with an excellent command of the Italian language, Austin Parke Goddard, a personal friend of the Grand Duke of Tuscany, Cosimo III. His version, first printed in 1753 - 1756, went into three editions.[15] It omitted as spurious, however, the disputed sections of Books Three and Four.

Spanish translations of the history were less numerous and less important, primarily because the close ties between Spain and Italy during the sixteenth and seventeenth centuries increased the likelihood that an educated Spaniard could read Italian works in the original language. Guicciardini's history would have certainly been of great interest to such people, since much of its content dealt with some of the most glorious military and political exploits of that young nation. The first translation, although it included only the first seven books, appeared in 1581 in the translation of Antonio Florez de Benavides; another partial version by Oton Edilo was published in 1683.[16] The most interesting indication of the esteem Spaniards had for the history is an edition and translation prepared by none other than the Spanish monarch himself, King Philip IV (1603 - 1665). The king wished to learn Italian, and he chose Guicciardini's history because he considered him to be the foremost of all Italian historians. This translation was not published until 1889, but it was apparently known by contemporaries of the king.

Perhaps the strangest of all the versions of this history was a sixteenth-century publication by an Italian, Captain Girolamo Borri di Arezzo. So taken was Borri by the dramatic sweep of the work and by the historical importance of its contents that he decided to transform the entire history into an epic poem. The result was a work even longer than the history itself! Needless to say, the poem had little success and was never published; it is now accessible only in manuscript form in the Laurentian Library in Florence.[17]

The résumé of the various translations of Guicciardini's historical masterpiece examined here is an incomplete one, one not intended to duplicate the more detailed studies of Vincenzo Luciani and Paolo Guicciardini. As their works have shown, an accurate picture of Guicciardini's reception abroad in translation necessitates a separate book. It is clear, however, from the body of evidence that these scholars have painstakingly amassed that Guicciardini was an extremely popular historical author not only in his own era but also during the Reformation and the eighteenth century, both ages that valued good historical narrative very highly. Very few Italian authors, with the possible exception of Machiavelli and Petrarch, enjoyed an equal exposure abroad during the same period. In spite of the fact that much of the interest in Guicciardini was derived from a self-serving search for anti-Catholic propaganda, many of Europe's greatest minds during the four centuries after its initial publication read the work and reacted to it in important ways. Through their response to his history, Guicciardini was indirectly to influence many others who had perhaps never seen the original work.

III   *Guicciardini and European Renaissance Thought*

One of the first important evaluations of Guicciardini's merits as a historian is located in Jean Bodin's *Method for the Easy Comprehension of History*, published in Latin in 1566. Although Bodin today is remembered especially for his formulation of the doctrine of sovereignty in his *Six Books of the Republic* (1576), his earlier work on the nature and uses of history had seemingly attained a greater popularity. By 1650, thirteen Latin editions had appeared in print. In an age which valued history and historical narrative even more than fiction, a judgment of the contribution of one of Europe's major historians was of crucial importance. Bodin clearly ranks Guicciardini above most, if not all, historians after the classical period, calling him "that very father of history," and wonders whether he did not, in fact, even excel the classical historians.[18] He is particularly impressed with Guicciardini's scrupulous accuracy and his regard for detail:

For where anything came under deliberation which seemed inexplicable, just there he showed the keenest subtlety in discussion, and everywhere he sprinkled sage opinions appropriately like salt. . . . Moreover, his zeal for ferreting out the truth was remarkable. He affirmed nothing rashly, but with all needful proofs. He is said to have extracted and interpreted letters, decrees, alliances, and speeches from the sources. . . . He was such a diligent investigator of matters, places, and persons, and even of plans and deeds, that he seems to have inspected thoroughly all the towns of Italy, municipia, camps, rivers, and what I think most important, the official records.[19]

Bodin is one of the first critics to direct attention to Guicciardini's historical method. Had he been appraised of the informaion contained in the historian's archives, he would have been even more impressed with Guicciardini's historical method which heralded a new age of modern historical investigation.

Bodin's advice to the reading public was to carry substantial weight, for Guicciardini's *History of Italy* became popular reading fare in France. One of the most prominent Frenchmen to comment upon the history was Montaigne. An avid and eclectic reader, the inventor of the essay discusses Guicciardini in one of his most substantial chapters, "On Books." His opinion is, however, a mixed one:

Here is what I put some ten years ago in my Guicciardini (for whatever language my books speak, I speak to them in my own): "He is a diligent historiographer from whom, in my opinion, one can learn the truth about the affairs of his time as exactly as from any other: and indeed in most of them he was an actor himself, and of honorable rank. There is no appearance that through hatred, favor, or vanity, he disguised things; which is attested by the free judgments he gives of the great, and especially of those by whom he had been advanced and employed in responsibilities, like Pope Clement VII."[20]

Montaigne praises Guicciardini for his lack of historical prejudice, but as a prose stylist of the Senecan variety, he felt that the majestic Ciceronian periods of Guicciardini's history contained too many digressions and discourses and that Guicciardini was "too fond of them"; "for by not wanting to leave anything unsaid, having a subject so full and ample and almost infinite, he becomes diffuse and smacking a bit of scholastic prattle."[21] His most damaging criticism, one which would be repeated many times by others, was directed at the key concept underlying Guicciardini's analytical method, his use of the concept of self-interest to explain much of human behavior:

I have also noted this, that of so many souls and actions that he judges, so many motives and plans, he never refers a single one to virtue, religion, and conscience, as if these qualities were wholly extinct in the world; and of all actions, however fair in appearance they may be of themselves, he throws the cause back onto some vicious motive or some profit. It is impossible to imagine that among the infinite number of actions that he judges there was not a single one produced by the way of reason. No corruption can have seized men so universally that someone would not escape the contagion. This makes me fear that his taste was a bit corrupted; and it may have happened that he judged others by himself.[22]

Such an objection struck at the heart of Guicciardini's approach to historical events and is a bit exaggerated. But Montaigne was correct when he observed that Guicciardini often underrated complex causes of a more subjective nature in his depiction of Italian history. His sensibility could understand chance and selfishness more than faith, charity, and kindness. Nevertheless, as Guicciardini might himself have replied, had there been more of these admirable qualities in abundance during the epoch described in *The History of Italy*, he would have been obliged to portray them as factors influencing the course of events. Unhappily, as he might have observed, Montaigne's objection was founded more upon wishful thinking than upon the realities of the Italian political scene.

Guicciardini was not without admirers in Renaissance England. Gabriel Harvey (c. 1545 - 1630), a close friend of Edmund Spenser, considered Guicciardini's *History of Italy* one of the best of all historical works (a "silver history"), and he favorably compared Guicciardini to Sallust, Livy, and Tacitus.[23] Sir Walter Raleigh (1552 - 1618) apparently utilized the history as a source book for his own *History of the World*.[24] More important, however, was the extensive influence Guicciardini exerted upon the works of Sir Francis Bacon.[25] It is interesting to note that Bacon, and many others, constantly availed themselves of Guicciardini's *History of Italy* as a source of moral and political exempla, although the idea of didacticism in history had already been largely abandoned by Guicciardini himself. In a great number of his works Bacon refers to incidents previously elucidated by Guicciardini: *Advertisement Touching the Controversies of the Church of England* (c. 1589); *Certain Observations Made Upon a Libel Published This Present Year, 1592; Advancement of Learning* (1605); *De Augmentis Scientiarum* (1623); *Considerations Touching a War with Spain* (1624); *Apophtlegmes New and Old* (1625); and *The Essayes or Counsels, Civill and Morall* (1625). As Luciani has pointed out, Bacon's *History of Henry VII* adopts not only Guicciardini's political conception of historiography, but it also imitates the use of character sketches and patterned speeches from that work.[26] Francis Bacon was also the writer who first rendered into English Guicciardini's crucial concept of the balance of power, which he had formulated first in the unpublished *History of Florence* and later in the opening chapter of *The History of Italy*. Guicciardini's *History of Italy* was the first modern book to propose this method for the analysis of international politics, one which has been consistently used since his day.[27] Bacon accepts the idea as the one basic rule necessary for a ruler to follow in his relations with his neighbors:

There can no general rule be given (the occasions are so variable), save one, which ever holdeth, neighbours do overgrow so (by increase of territory, by embracing of trade, by approaches, or the like) as they become more able to annoy them than they were. . . . During that triumvirate of kings, King

Henry the Eighth of England, Francis the First King of France, and Charles the Fifth Emperor, there was such a watch kept that none of the three could win a palm of ground, but the other two would straightways balance it, either by confederation or, if need were, by a war, and would not in any wise take up peace at interest. And the like was done by that league (which Guicciardini saith was the security of Italy) made between Ferdinando, King of Naples, Lorenzius Medices, and Ludovicus Sforza, potentates, the one of Florence, the other of Milan.[28]

Historical or philosophical writers were not the only ones attracted to Guicciardini's historical masterpiece. John Milton favorably refers to Guicciardini in his commonplace book.[29] At least one play, Barnabe Barnes's *The Devil's Charter* (1606), was taken from material in *The History of Italy*. Guicciardini appears as a character in the work's prologue in a role not unlike that assigned to Machiavelli by Christopher Marlowe in *The Jew of Malta*.[30] This does not compare to the tremendous impact Machiavelli had upon Elizabethan drama, where "Machiavellian" villains came to be a commonplace phenomenon based upon a gross misconception of the nature of *The Prince* or of its author. Guicciardini, unlike Machiavelli, never penetrated into the popular imagination as a personality in his own right, but his work enjoyed widespread esteem, and many episodes related in the history became legendary in English tradition as well as in Italian. Two editions of Chomedey's French translation of the history contained sonnets by Pierre de Ronsard and Jean-Antoine de Baif, both major poets of the French Renaissance. They praise either Guicciardini's merits as a truthful, unbiased historian or Chomedey's achievement as a translator of so important a work.[31] Guicciardini's appeal has always been to the intellect rather than to the emotions, and his works never generated the kind of literary reaction that occurred when Renaissance poets encountered other Italian writers.

Guicciardini's reputation and influence grew during the years of religious strife in Europe. Protestants sought to use his history to substantiate their appeal for church reform, while Catholics repudiated as incorrect and biased Guicciardini's revelations of ecclesiastical corruption in high places. Several Italian and Latin editions were placed on the *Index librorum prohibitorum*.[32] However, translations in various languages (German, Dutch, French, and English) were never prohibited, even though they were published in countries far more susceptible to Protestant propagandists. Since no Italian edition contained the disputed passages from Books Three, Four, Six, and Ten until they were included in the so-called Fribourg edition of 1775 - 1776, actually printed in Florence with a German place of publication to confuse the censors, the explanation for banning only selected editions of *The History of Italy* escapes reason. Indubitably, those who banned the book had access to some of the manuscript copies in circulation which contained those passages. Innumerable partial editions in many languages of any and all sections of the history that might be damaging to the Catholic cause were published in every Protestant country from the sixteenth to the nineteenth centuries. Guicciardini's historical methods and his unerring emphasis upon self-interest as the key to the meaning of human activity found a worthy successor in the Reformation historian Paolo Sarpi. In his *History of Benefices* (1675) and the *History of the Council of Trent* (1619), written during the height of the controversy over church reform in Italy, Sarpi examines the process whereby the church acquired and was corrupted by its wealth as well as the political motivations behind the Council of Trent and its Counter-Reformation decrees. Protestants tended to use both Guicciardini and Sarpi in their war of words with the church in Rome, and at least one edition appeared in England which contained not only a translation of Sarpi's *History of the Council of Trent* but also the sensitive passages from Books Three, Four, and Ten in Guicciardini's *History of Italy*.[33]

IV   The Battle of the Books

During the seventeenth and eighteenth centuries in Europe, the literary world was split apart by a controversy known to us today as "the Battle of the Books." The origin of this both literary and philosophical quarrel was the argument over the relationship of the modern era to that of classical antiquity. Renaissance poets and artists had usually proclaimed their desire to imitate, emulate, and to equal the ancients. This feeling had sometimes degenerated into a slavish worship of the authority and tradition of the past, but numerous great artists had been able to avoid sterility in their inspiration from the classical writers and artists. Nevertheless, the issue over the alleged universal superiority of the classics in cultural matters had to be squarely faced sooner or later. Because the rebirth of interest in the classics had begun first in Italy, it was only fitting that the first skirmishes in "the Battle of the Books" began there

with a long and heated debate concerning the relative merits of
Italian epic poems and their classical models. Alessandro Tassoni
(1565 - 1635), better known for his mock-epic *The Captured Bucket*,
published one of the earliest attacks upon the authority of the
classics, his *Miscellaneous Thoughts* (1620).[34] Later in France, the
issue was joined in earnest with Charles Perrault's *Parallel between
the Ancients and the Moderns* which appeared between 1688 and
1697. Perrault's staunch defense of the superiority of the moderns
was very influential. It helped to spark a similar debate in England
and caused a sharp argument with Boileau, the defender of French
classicism. In England, the argument was taken up by Jonathan
Swift in *The Battle of the Books* (1704), from which the controversy
derives its English label.

Guicciardini's reputation as a historian plays a small but significant role in this literary debate. For years, his *History of Italy* had
been considered one of the foremost historical narratives written in a
vernacular tongue, a book worthy to stand as a successor to such
classical writers as Thucydides, Livy, and Herodotus. The comparison was usually quite muted, however, and Guicciardini's
humanist predecessors would have been horrified to have even
thought of such an idea, since the classical writers were for them
models whose elegance of Latin style and exemplary figures of virtue or valor could be imitated but not surpassed. Progress in the arts
thus meant restoring the original supremacy of the ancients, not going beyond their achievements. The very fact that both Machiavelli
and Guicciardini chose to compose their histories in Italian, and not
the learned Latin of the tradition to which they belonged and which
they were trying to modify, emphasizes their perhaps unconscious
desire to align themselves with those who believed in the possibility
of some progress in the arts.

Perrault's *Parallel between the Ancients and the Moderns* clearly
states that historians like Guicciardini, Paolo Sarpi, and others could
easily be compared in rank to Thucydides or Livy.[35] Swift's *Battle of
the Books* seems to reply directly to this assertion, for in that satiric
depiction of an actual battle between the two groups of writers,
Guicciardini is included in a rather unflattering description: "There
came several bodies of heavy-armed foot, all mercenaries, under the
ensigns of Guicciardini, Davila, Polydore Virgil, Buchanan,
Mariana, Camden, and others."[36] Although the outcome of such a
battle was clear in Swift's mind, his opinion was not shared by
succeeding generations. The end result of "the Battle of the Books"

was, among other things, a general agreement that the Moderns could rival the Ancients or even transcend their achievements.

This sentiment seems to have been accepted by several major eighteenth-century historians, at least in the matter of Guicciardini's historical merits. Viscount Bolingbroke ventured to assert in his important *Letters on the Study and Use of History* (1752) that he preferred "Guicciardini to Thucydides in every respect."[37] Others may not have agreed with this strong statement, but they concurred in the feeling that Guicciardini merited equal consideration with the best Roman and Greek historians. Edward Gibbon ranks Guicciardini and Thucydides together as having lived "in the true Station of historians of their own times" since both had "personal knowledge of great men."[38] Voltaire agreed with Gibbon's assessment of Guicciardini's excellence as a historian because of his proximity to the events he described, saying that "Italy had, in Guicciardini, its Thucydides, or rather its Xenophon, since he sometimes commanded in the wars he described."[39] Voltaire, incidentally, is one of the first historians to attack as erroneous Guicciardini's description of the death of Pope Alexander VI and the nearly fatal illness of Cesare Borgia. Paradoxically, this severe critic of the church himself comes to the defense of historical truth in this instance. Stranger still, however, is the fact that while Guicciardini's description of this single incident in Book Three of *The History of Italy* is rejected, other more damaging tales of the Borgias' transgressions are assumed to be authentic and are even embellished. Voltaire reports, for instance, Guicciardini's version of the incestuous relationships between the members of the family, comparing Cesare Borgia to Tamerlane and other ferocious oriental rulers in evildoing, and he describes what he calls the unparalleled debauchery at Lucrezia Borgia's wedding to the Duke of Este where, he claims, fifty nude courtesans danced for the papal court and its "incestuous family" while prizes were given to those with the most licentious movements![40] It is difficult to explain why Voltaire believed only a part of this legend, but a single disagreement with his source did not diminish his admiration for the complete work.

V *New Views in the Nineteenth Century*

The publication of the Canestrini edition of Guicciardini's complete works in the nineteenth century sparked a new interest in the writer. For the first time, scholars realized that Guicciardini was not just the author of *The History of Italy*. The complete final version of

the *Ricordi* appeared for the first time in print along with numerous
political dialogues and discourses, autobiographical works, the first
History of Florence, and the *Considerations on the 'Discourses' of
Machiavelli.* Previously, students of the Italian Renaissance had
been confronted with the author of a single, although very important history, as well as a fragmentary collection of maxims, but now
they were faced with what amounted to an enormous collection of
works which had gone completely unanalyzed in any study of the
historical and political literature of the period. Furthermore, even
received opinions about the place of the works already known to
have been written by Guicciardini had to be modified in the light of
the new writings. A further surprise lay in store for Guicciardini
scholars in the twentieth century when a second, unsuspected
history of Florence, *Florentine Affairs,* was published in 1945.

With the discovery of so much essential information about their
past suddenly unearthed, it was only natural that the Italians of the
Risorgimento would wish to reexamine their traditions in the light of
their recent struggle for national independence and unification. Particular attention was paid to the Renaissance during this period of
national soul-searching, for educated Italians wanted to know why
Italy had reached such a pinnacle of achievement in every possible
area in that period and had, at the same time, lost its political independence to foreign powers. What inherent weakness in the
Italian character, many asked, could have caused such a disaster?
Out of this questioning came one of the most influential interpretations of Francesco Guicciardini's works, that of the literary
historian Francesco De Sanctis (1817 - 1883).

De Sanctis discusses Guicciardini in two major critical articles: an
essay entitled "L'uomo del Guicciardini" which appeared in his
Saggi critici in 1865; and a chapter entitled "Machiavelli" in his
magisterial *History of Italian Literature.* Although De Sanctis admits that *The History of Italy,* judged by the "standard of intellectual power . . . must be classed as the most important work that has
ever issued from the Italian mind," he studies Guicciardini essentially from the vantage point of the *Ricordi.*[41] In fact, his essay in
Saggi critici was written in reaction to his reading of Canestrini's
partially completed edition of the complete works which had
recently appeared. De Sanctis thus represents a more contemporary
interpretation of Guicciardini in that he elevates the book of maxims
and philosophical reflections to a level of parity, if not supremacy,
with the better known history. De Sanctis felt that Renaissance

Italians had abandoned spiritual values, the ability to sacrifice themselves for a cause, the love of liberty and freedom, for a life based upon self-interest, Guicciardini's *particulare.* Like Machiavelli, Guicciardini wanted Italy to be freed from the barbarians and from the influence of the priests, but unlike Machiavelli, Guicciardini felt these things in his intellect, not in his heart, and would not act against his own self - interest:

Machiavelli struggled against the corruption of Italy, and did not despair of his country; he had the illusions of a noble heart; he belonged to that earlier generation of Florentine patriots who in the midst of all the ruin searched for some cure for it and were not resigned, and did honour to Italy in their failure. With Guicciardini appears a generation that is already resigned. He has no illusions. And seeing no remedy for the corruption, he wraps himself up in it, makes use of it for his sagacity, and makes it into his aureole. His *Ricordi* are nothing else than the Italian corruption made into a code and promoted to be the rule of life.[42]

Like so many other Risorgimento Italians, De Sanctis shared the belief that Machiavelli's exhortation at the end of *The Prince* to rid Italy of the barbarians was a spiritual forerunner of their battle for national unification, and Guicciardini's willingness to compromise his personal inclinations for his own self-interest did not suit a generation which had been tested in prison, exile, and war to achieve independence. Furthermore, De Sanctis saw the particular intellectual position of Guicciardini as a kind of perennial Italian outlook, still present in Italian life and still harmful to the welfare of the nation state:

Italy perished because the fools were too few and the wise men were too many. Cities, princes, and the people all responded to the model stupendously outlined in these *Ricordi.* The ideal was no longer Farinata but the Medici; the writer of these times was no longer Dante but Francesco Guicciardini. . . . Country, religion, liberty, honor, glory, all that moves men to magnanimous deeds and makes nations great, although admitted in theory, no longer had any meaning in practical life, no longer were the motivation of social life. . . . An individual like our sage [i.e. Guicciardini] can perhaps live, but a society cannot.[43]

De Sanctis further asserts that Guicciardini's model of man can be met at every step in the Italy of his day, and he warns that "this fatal man hinders our path, if we do not have the strength to kill him in our consciousness."[44]

VI   A Contemporary Assessment

Our picture of Francesco Guicciardini and the central place his historical and political works occupy in the Italian and European Renaissance need no longer be clouded by the antipathy De Sanctis felt for the man himself. Through the labors of several generations of scholars, the twentieth-century reader is better equipped than previous generations to consult all of Guicciardini's works and to reconstruct an accurate idea of how his works developed and how they were nurtured by the political and historical events of his times. Most contemporary students of the Renaissance would agree with John R. Hale's estimation of Guicciardini's stature as "the greatest historian between Tacitus in the first century and Voltaire and Gibbon in the eighteenth and he is one of the greatest of all writers of contemporary history."[45] As the author of the *Ricordi*, the *Considerations on the 'Discourses' of Machiavelli*, and numerous dialogues and treatises, Guicciardini merits increased recognition as one of the most original philosophical minds of his day. His major historical works provide us with an incomparable view of the central events and the colorful heros and villains of one of the most exciting moments in the history of the human spirit. Guicciardini was part of "that wondrous Florentine spirit," as Jacob Burckhardt put it in his monumental *Civilization of the Renaissance in Italy*, "at once keenly critical and artistically creative" which "incessantly transformed the social and political condition of the State, and just as incessantly described and judged the change. Florence thus became the home of political doctrines and theories, of experiments and sudden changes . . . and alone and above all other States in the world, the home of historical representation in the modern sense of the phrase."[46] Without the contribution of Francesco Guicciardini, Burckhardt's famous assertion would have little meaning. It is probably hopeless to wish that Guicciardini might receive the same attention that his illustrious counterpart and friend, Niccolò Machiavelli, has received in the past four centuries. He was detached, aloof, and too proud to associate with those he considered beneath his own intellectual plane or his social status. Many of his contemporaries, and not a few of his readers, mistakenly viewed this quality as a result of a personal meanness or some secret flaw in his character and were, unlike the more perspicacious Machiavelli, unwilling to penetrate past this to come to grips with the important historical, political, and philosophical issues discussed in his many writings. If we cannot harbor affection for the man, we should nevertheless be able to admire his work and the sharp intellect that produced it. For in many ways, and not the least in this ambivalent reaction commonly produced in those who study him, Francesco Guicciardini was so much a product of the culture that he portrayed and so representative a part of it that we cannot claim to understand that complex intellectual, historical, and cultural phenomenon we label the Italian Renaissance without making his life and writings a part of our own historical consciousness.

Notes and References

Chapter One

1. For recent archival studies on the background of Guicciardini's family, see Richard A. Goldthwaite, *Private Wealth in Renaissance Florence: A Study of Four Families* (Princeton, 1968), pp. 108 - 55; or Randolph Starn, "Francesco Guicciardini and His Brothers," in *Renaissance Studies in Honor of Hans Baron*, eds. Anthony Molho and John A. Tedeschi (Dekalb, 1971), pp. 407 - 44. Much of the discussion on Guicciardini's life in this chapter is indebted to the indispensable biography by Roberto Ridolfi, *The Life of Francesco Guicciardini*, trans. Cecil Grayson (New York, 1968). The gonfaloniere, or standard bearer, was the most important officer of the Florentine government, the chief executive of the Republic. The Signoria was the most important lawmaking body of the Republic, for only this institution could initiate legislation. Depending upon the era in question, the Florentine Signoria consisted of from six to eight Priors, elected by a combination of direct votes or choice by lot.

2. *Francesco Guicciardini: Selected Writings*, ed. Cecil Grayson and trans. Margaret Grayson (London, 1965), p. 132. All future references to the *Ricordanze*, as well as those to the *Considerations on the 'Discourses' of Machiavelli*, will be taken from this translation unless otherwise indicated.

3. Cited from *Memorie di famiglia* in *Scritti autobiografici e rari*, ed. Roberto Palmarocchi (Bari, 1956), p. 3.

4. *Selected Writings*, p. 130.

5. Ibid., p. 133.

6. Ibid., p. 134.

7. Ibid., p. 144.

8. Ridolfi, *Life of Guicciardini*, p. viii.

9. Quoted from Francesco Vettori's *Storia d'Italia* by Ridolfi, *Life of Guicciardini*, p. 124.

10. For the best discussion of the political and economic factors involved in the transition from a republic to a principality in Florence, see Rudolf von Albertini, *Firenze dalla repubblica al principato: storia e coscienza politica*, trans. Cesare Cristofolini (Turin, 1970); see also Felix Gilbert, *Machiavelli*

and Guicciardini: Politics and History in Sixteenth-Century Florence
(Princeton, 1965), pp. 7 - 152.

11. Cited by Ridolfi, *Life of Guicciardini,* p. 211.

12. Typical of this interpretation is that very influential essay by
Francesco De Sanctis, "L'uomo del Guicciardini," which will be discussed
in another chapter.

13. Ridolfi, *Life of Guicciardini,* pp. 248 - 49.

14. Ibid., p. 274.

Chapter Two

1. The critical edition of the original Italian text is found in Roberto
Palmarocchi, ed., *Storie fiorentine* (Bari, 1931); Giuseppe Canestrini's first
edition appeared in 1859 with a slightly different title. For the only complete English edition of this work available, from which all citations are
taken, see the excellent translation by Mario Domandi, *The History of
Florence* (New York, 1970). Domandi's translation also includes a very
useful glossary of technical terms referring to various aspects of Florentine
government (pp. xxxix - xlvii). For a good introduction to the place of *The
History of Florence* in the tradition of humanist historiography as well as an
excellent edition of portions of both major historical works by Guicciardini,
see *The History of Italy and The History of Florence,* trans. Cecil Grayson
with an introduction by J. H. Hale (New York, 1964).

2. *History of Florence,* p. 1.

3. Ibid., p. 8.

4. Nicolai Rubinstein, "The *Storie fiorentine* and the *Memorie di
famiglia* by Francesco Guicciardini," *Rinascimento* 4 (1953), 193 - 219.

5. Ibid., p. 218. For a thorough discussion of Savonarola's contributions
to Renaissance political theory, see Donald Weinstein, *Savonarola and
Florence: Prophecy and Patriotism in the Renaissance* (Princeton: Princeton
University Press, 1970), pp. 289 - 316.

6. For discussions of humanist historiography in Florence before Guic-
ciardini or Machiavelli, see Felix Gilbert, *Machiavelli and Guicciardini,* pp.
203 - 36 and passim; Donald Wilcox, *The Development of Florentine
Humanist Historiography in the Fifteenth Century* (Cambridge: Harvard
University Press, 1969); Peter Burke, *The Renaissance Sense of the Past*
(New York: St. Martin's, 1969); and Nancy S. Struever, *The Language of
History in the Renaissance: Rhetoric and Historical Consciousness in
Florentine Humanism* (Princeton: Princeton University Press, 1970).

7. Gilbert, ibid., p. 225.

8. Felix Gilbert, "Guicciardini, Machiavelli, Valori on Lorenzo
Magnifico," *Renaissance Quarterly* 11 (1958), 109, discusses this typical
technique and its use in three portraits of Lorenzo. He notes the existence of
a portrait of Lorenzo not inserted in any of Guicciardini's histories which, in

contrast to the critical treatment of the man in *The History of Florence*, is highly favorable to Lorenzo, having been written much later in Guicciardini's career when his allegiances and obligations to the Medici house had become stronger. For a general treatment of the functions of the character sketch in other contemporary historical works, see my own *Machiavelli and the Art of Renaissance History* (Detroit, 1973).

9. Ridolfi, *Life of Guicciardini*, p. 22.

10. *Selected Writings*, p. 37.

11. *History of Florence*, p. 3.

12. Ibid., p. 4.

13. Ibid., p. 75.

14. Gilbert, *Machiavelli and Guicciardini*, p. 60ff., contains an excellent analysis of this phenomenon.

15. *History of Florence*, p. 192.

16. Ibid., p. 271.

17. Gilbert, *Machiavelli and Guicciardini*, pp. 255 - 67, discusses this development in histories written not only by Guicciardini but also in Bernardino Corio's *History of Milan* (1503), Bernardo Rucellai's *History of the French Invasion* (published only in 1724), and Girolamo Borgia's *History of the Italian Wars* (completed in 1544 and never actually published). Guicciardini would later use both Rucellai and Borgia as sources for his *History of Italy*.

18. *History of Florence*, pp. 88 - 89.

19. Ibid., p. 69.

20. Ibid., p. 77.

21. Ibid., p. 76. Other historical accounts of Lorenzo's physical appearance, Machiavelli's, for instance, agree with Guicciardini's assessment; it is therefore not motivated by his distaste for Lorenzo's policies.

22. Ibid.

23. Machiavelli, *Lettere*, ed. Franco Gaeta (Milan: Feltrinelli, 1961), p. 33. All translations of the letters of Machiavelli or those from Guicciardini to Machiavelli included in this study are my own.

24. *History of Florence*, pp. 104, 106.

25. These papers, known as the *Estratti savonaroliani*, have never been translated; they are included in *Scritti autobiografici e rari*, pp. 285 - 333.

26. *History of Florence*, p. 146.

27. Ibid., p. 148.

28. Rubinstein, "The *Storie fiorentine* and the *Memorie di famiglia*" pp. 186 - 90.

29. This interpretation is suggested by Vittorio De Caprariis, *Francesco Guicciardini: dalla politica alla storia* (Bari, 1950), p. 61, and is accepted by von Albertini, *Firenze dalla repubblica al principato*, p. 87. Arguments against this position are offered by Felix Gilbert, "The Renaissance Interest in History," in *Art, Science, and History in the Renaissance*, ed. Charles S.

Singleton (Baltimore: Johns Hopkins University Press, 1967), pp. 380 - 81;
Rubinstein, ibid., pp. 171 - 72; and by Emanuella Lugnani Scarano in the
introduction to *Opere di Francesco Guicciardini* (Turin, 1970), p. 42.

Chapter Three

1. The Italian titles are respectively *Diario del viaggio in Spagna;
Relazione di Spagna; Del governo di Firenze dopo la restaurazione de'
Medici nel 1512; Del modo di assicurare lo stato alla casa de' Medici; Discorso di Logrogno* (also known as *Del modo di ordinare il governo popolare*);
and *Dialogo del Reggimento di Firenze.* The critical editions of the first two
works are found in *Scritti autobiografici e rari*, pp. 103 - 46. The other
dialogues and discourses are found in *Dialogo e discorsi del Reggimento di
Firenze*, ed. Roberto Palmarocchi (Bari, 1932), pp. 3 - 172, 218 - 81. Since
both of these critical editions are currently out of print and are often difficult
to locate, I cite only the minor dialogues from them. The same critical texts
of the two most important works, the *Discourse of Logrogno* and the
Dialogue on the Government of Florence, are reproduced in the previously
cited edition, *Opere di Francesco Guicciardini*, ed. Emanuella Lugnani
Scarano, pp. 247 - 483. I therefore take all quotations of these two works
from this later edition. All translations of these dialogues are my own.

2. For a study of Guicciardini's various assessments of Spain in his works,
see Vincenzo Luciani, "Il Guicciardini e la Spagna," *PMLA* 56 (1941), 992 -
1106.

3. Von Albertini, *Firenze dalla repubblica al principato*, pp. 3 - 103, contains an excellent discussion of this interrelation and also presents the unpublished texts of several of these works by such men as Paolo Vettori, Goro
Gheri, Lodovico Alamanni, and Niccolò Guicciardini (Francesco's nephew).

4. See Gilbert, *Machiavelli and Guicciardini*, pp. 84 - 87, for a discussion
of this problem.

5. For the place of Venice in Florentine political thought, see Felix
Gilbert, "The Venetian Constitution in Florentine Political Thought," in
Florentine Studies: Politics and Society in Renaissance Florence, ed. Nicolai
Rubinstein (Evanston: Northwestern University Press, 1968), pp. 463 - 500;
and J. G. A. Pocock, *The Machiavellian Moment: Florentine Political
Thought and the Atlantic Republican Tradition* (Princeton, 1975), pp. 83 -
113, 183 - 330.

6. Von Albertini, *Firenze dalla repubblica al principato*, p. 9.

7. Ibid., p. 10.

8. *Opere di Francesco Guicciardini*, p. 254; Pocock, *The Machiavellian
Moment*, pp. 124 - 25, believes that this definition of political power can be
"easily misunderstood" if it is taken to refer to political power in general;
Pocock contends that the term I have translated as "state and empire" ("lo
stato e lo imperio") refers to "external power, the power of the city over
those not of the city, such as the Florentines sought over the stubbornly

resisting Pisans. The implication is not that the authority exercised by Florentines over Florentines is a species of violence, but rather that it is or may be the only sort of authority which is not." While the implication of the term *lo imperio* would seem to substantiate his distinction between internal power without violence in *lo stato* as opposed to external power based upon nothing but violence in *lo imperio*, the term *stato* in the political vocabulary of the period has never been shown to have this exclusively external connotation. On the contrary, the many studies of the term in the political treatises of the period view the word *stato* as a flexible term which generally referred to the reins of government or access to power within the city - state. For various studies of this term, see Nicolai Rubinstein, "Notes on the word *stato* in Florence before Machiavelli," in *Florilegium Historiale: Essays Presented to Wallace K. Ferguson*, eds. J. G. Rowe and W. H. Stockdale (Toronto: University of Toronto Press, 1971), pp. 314 - 26; J. H. Hexter, *The Vision of Politics on the Eve of the Reformation: More, Machiavelli, and Seyssel* (New York: Basic Books, 1973); Felix Gilbert, *Machiavelli and Guicciardini*, pp. 326 - 30; and Fredi Chiappelli, *Studi sul linguaggio del Machiavelli* (Florence: Biblioteca del saggiatore, 1952). The maxim that Pocock cites from Guicciardini as support for his position (C - 48) states that the *origin* of political power is always in violence except in the case of republics, but this remark is not intended to be taken as a definition of the *nature* or *essence* of political power, as is clearly Guicciardini's statement in the *Discourse of Logrogno*.

9. Ibid., p. 255.

10. Ibid., p. 257.

11. Ibid., p. 294.

12. Ibid., p. 250; Pocock, *The Machiavellian Moment*, pp. 123, 137 - 38, also analyzes these similes within the context of Guicciardini's views on political reform.

13. *Dialogo e discorsi*, p. 276.

14. Ibid.

15. Emanuella Lugnani Scarano, "Il dialogo *Del Reggimento di Firenze* di Francesco Guicciardini," *Giornale storico della letteratura italiana* 145 (1968), 260.

16. Pocock, *The Machiavellian Moment*, pp. 140, 150.

17. Ridolfi, *Life of Guicciardini*, p. 136.

18. Scarano, "Il dialogo *Del Reggimento di Firenze* di Francesco Guicciardini," p. 537.

19. Ibid., p. 292ff. The specific version of the *Ricordi* reflected in the *Dialogue on the Government of Florence* is the second one (known as version A). For a detailed discussion of the various constitutional reforms discussed in this work, see Pocock, *The Machiavellian Moment*, pp. 219 - 71.

20. *Opere di Francesco Guicciardini*, p. 367.

21. Ibid., p. 336.

22. Ibid., p. 354.

23. Ibid.
24. Ibid.
25. Ibid., p. 355.
26. De Caprariis, *Francesco Guicciardini: dalla politica alla storia*, p. 86.
27. Gilbert, *Machiavelli and Guicciardini*, p. 234.
28. The utopian aspects of the *Dialogue on the Government of Florence* are discussed by De Caprariis, *Francesco Guicciardini: dalla politica alla storia*, p. 81, and by Scarano, "Il dialogo *Del Reggimento di Firenze* di Francesco Guicciardini," pp. 238 - 39.

Chapter Four

1. All translations of these three works are my own and are taken from the previously cited *Opere di Francesco Guicciardini*, ed. Scarano, which reprints the critical editions contained in *Scritti autobiografici e rari*.
2. *Life of Guicciardini*, p. 184.
3. *Opere di Francesco Guicciardini*, p. 492.
4. Ibid., p. 500.
5. Although Scarano (ibid., p. 49) claims that one cannot determine with accuracy Guicciardini's intent, Ridolfi (*Life of Guicciardini*, p. 313) demonstrates clearly that Guicciardini's problems with the republic after 1527 had nothing to do with the charges discussed in the three works; consequently, no practical purpose is possible. To use Machiavelli's favorite term, the two speeches are *ghiribizzi* or products of the imagination.
6. *Opere di Francesco Guicciardini*, pp. 518, 523.
7. Emanuella Lugnani Scarano, "Le redazioni dei *Ricordi* e la storia del pensiero politico guicciardiniano dal 1512 al 1530," *Giornale storico della letteratura italiana* 147 (1970), 227.
8. *Opere di Francesco Guicciardini*, p. 534.
9. Ibid., p. 532.

Chapter Five

1. Ridolfi, *Life of Guicciardini*, p. 208.
2. *Selected Writings*, p. 108.
3. *The Prince and the Discourses* (New York: Random House, 1950), pp. 151 - 52.
4. *Selected Writings*, p. 81.
5. Ibid.
6. Ibid., p. 96.
7. Ibid., pp. 105, 103.
8. Ibid., p. 68.
9. Ugo Spirito, *Machiavelli e Guicciardini* (Florence, 1945), p. 76.
10. Ridolfi, *Life of Guicciardini*, p. 207.
11. Machiavelli, *Lettere*, p. 407.
12. Ibid., p. 417.

13. Ibid., p. 448.
14. Ibid., p. 505.
15. Cited by Ridolfi, *Life of Guicciardini,* p. 156.

Chapter Six

1. The original titles in full are as follows: *Più consigli et avvertimenti di M. Fr. Guicciardini Gentilhuomo fior. in materia di re publica et di privata* (Paris, 1576); *Considerazioni civili sopra l'Historie di M. Francesco Guicciardini e d'altri historici: Trattate per modo di discorso da M. Remigio Fiorentino* (Venice, 1582).

2. For the history of these translations, see Vincenzo Luciani, *Francesco Guicciardini e la fortuna dell'opera sua* (Florence, 1949), especially pp. 311 - 34.

3. Canestrini published both manuscripts together in Francesco Guicciardini, *Opere inedite* (Florence, 1857 - 1867), II, 81 - 224.

4. My remarks here synthesize a great many arguments. The reader who wishes to examine the details and conflicting points of view should consult the following works: Raffaele Spongano, *Ricordi, edizione critica* (Florence, 1951), pp. ix - lxxii; Michele Barbi, "Per una compiuta edizione dei *Ricordi politici e civili* del Guicciardini," *Studi di filologia italiana* 3 (1932), 163 - 96; Emanuella Lugnani Scarano, "Le redazioni dei *Ricordi* e la storia del pensiero guicciardiniano dal 1512 al 1530," pp. 183 - 259; Mario Fubini, "Le quattro redazioni dei *Ricordi* del Guicciardini (contributo allo studio della formazione del linguaggio e dello stile guicciardiniano), *Civiltà moderna* 13 (1941), 105 - 24, 247 - 71; and Francesco Guicciardini, *Scritti politici e Ricordi,* ed. Roberto Palmarocchi, pp. 369 - 79. An excellent discussion of this problem is fortunately available in English: see Mario Domandi's "Translator's Preface" in Francesco Guicciardini, *Maxims and Reflections (Ricordi)* (Philadelphia, 1972), pp. 35 - 38. I cite from this translation and not from the other available edition of the *Ricordi* by Cecil Grayson (included in *Selected Writings,* pp. 4 - 56), since Domandi's version contains both the C and B manuscript plus the early Q^1 and Q^2 *ricordi* as well as a very useful table comparing the various manuscripts.

5. The Guicciardini family archives are located in the Palazzo Guicciardini on Via Guicciardini which is still inhabited by the descendants of Francesco Guicciardini. The palazzo is adjacent to the more famous Palazzo Pitti which contains one of Italy's most important art collections. For an interesting study of this palace's history with illustrations, see Paolo Guicciardini and Emilio Dori, *Le antiche case ed il palazzo dei Guicciardini in Firenze* (Florence, 1952). The palazzo contains not only an archive with almost all of the extant autograph manuscripts of Guicciardini's many works but also another library where most of the various translations, editions, and works by or about Guicciardini and his family are preserved for consultation by scholars.

6. *The Prince and the Discourses,* p. 56.

7. *Maxims and Reflections,* p. 69.

8. Ibid., p. 71.

9. Ibid., p. 77.

10. Ibid., pp. 76 - 77.

11. Ibid., p. 70.

12. Ibid., p. 51.

13. Ibid., pp. 60 - 61.

14. *The Counter-Renaissance* (New York: Harcourt, 1950), pp. xi - xvii.

15. *Renaissance and Revolution: Backgrounds to Seventeenth-Century English Literature* (New York: Random House, 1967), p. 13.

16. Ibid., pp. 14 - 15.

17. Raffaello Ramat, *Il Guicciardini e la tragedia d'Italia* (Florence, 1953), p. 89.

18. *Maxims and Reflections,* p. 42.

19. Ibid., p. 43.

20. Ibid., p. 88.

21. Ibid., p. 43.

22. Ibid., p. 82.

23. Ibid., p. 75.

24. Ibid., p. 94.

25. Ibid., p. 72.

26. Ibid., pp. 72 - 73.

27. Ibid., p. 73.

28. Ibid., p. 92.

29. Ibid., pp. 56 - 57.

30. Ibid., p. 49.

31. Ibid.

32. Ibid., p. 89.

33. Ibid., p. 88.

34. Ibid., p. 101.

35. Ibid., pp. 125 - 26.

36. Ibid., p. 48.

37. Ibid., p. 97. Here, rather than "el particulare," the original Italian phrase translated as "their own interests" is "lo interesse proprio."

38. Ibid.

39. Ibid., p. 39.

40. Ibid.

41. *Saggi critici,* ed. Luigi Russo (Bari, 1965), III, 224.

42. *Maxims and Reflections,* p. 97.

43. Ibid., p. 95.

44. For an excellent analysis of this problem, see Corrado Rosso, *La 'Maxime': Saggi per una tipologia critica* (Naples: Edizioni scientifiche italiane, 1968).

45. *Maxims and Reflections,* p. 95.

46. See Emanuella Lugnani Scarano, "Le redazioni dei *Ricordi* e la storia del pensiero guicciardiniano dal 1512 al 1530," pp. 183 - 259.

47. Ibid., pp. 258 - 59. For a briefer presentation of Scarano's thesis, see her recent *Guicciardini e la crisi del Rinascimento* (Bari, 1973), especially pp. 61 - 84.

Chapter Seven

1. Gilbert, *Machiavelli and Guicciardini*, pp. 222 - 23. Gilbert's work contains the best account of humanist historiography available.

2. Bruni's *Historiae florentinae* and Bracciolini's *Historia florentina* were published in Latin respectively in 1610 and 1715; the Italian translations appeared in 1476 and again in 1492.

3. For an excellent discussion of the Italian medieval historians, see Louis Green, *Chronicle Into History* (Cambridge: Harvard University Press, 1972).

4. For the history of this discovery, see Francesco Guicciardini, *Le cose fiorentine ora per la prima volta pubblicate*, ed. Roberto Ridolfi (Florence, 1945), pp. xvii - xl. All citations from this work are taken from this edition; translations are my own.

5. Ibid., p. 55.

6. Ibid., p. 59.

7. Ibid., pp. 79 - 80.

8. John R. Hale, "Introduction," in Francesco Guicciardini, *History of Italy and History of Florence*, p. xvii.

Chapter Eight

1. *The History of Italy*, trans. Sidney Alexander (New York, 1969), p. 150. All future references to this work are taken from this edition.

2. Cited from Cicero, *De Oratore* (Book II, chapter 15) by Gilbert, *Machiavelli and Guicciardini*, p. 273; the original Latin of Guicciardini's text differs only slightly from the Loeb Library version cited by Gilbert and is reported by Robert Ridolfi in *Genesi della Storia d'Italia guicciardiniana* (Florence, 1939), p. 8.

3. *History of Italy*, p. 3.

4. Cited by Felix Gilbert in his "Saggio Introduttivo" to Francesco Guicciardini, *Storia d'Italia*, ed. Silvana Seidel Menchi (Turin, 1971), I, lix.

5. Ridolfi, *Life of Guicciardini*, p. 266.

6. *The History of Italian Literature*, trans. Joan Redfern (New York, 1959), II, 593.

7. *History of Italy*, p. 51.

8. Ibid., p. 56.

9. Ibid., p. 32.

10. Ibid., pp. 4, 7.

11. Ibid., p. 4.

12. For this interpretation, see Raffaello Ramat, *Il Guicciardini e la*

tragedia d'Italia, pp. 107 - 8; Felix Gilbert elaborates upon Ramat's thesis in *Machiavelli and Guicciardini*, pp. 285 - 87 and in his previously cited introduction to the Menchi edition of the *Storia d'Italia* (I, lxvii - lxix).

13. *History of Italy*, pp. 48 - 49.

14. Ibid., p. 3.

15. Ibid., p. 301.

16. Ibid., p. 3.

17. Ibid., p. 49.

18. Ibid., p. 273.

19. Ibid., p. 123.

20. Ibid., p. 124.

21. Ibid., p. 165.

22. Ibid.

23. Ibid., p. 166.

24. Ibid.

25. The best antidote to such historical misinterpretations is an excellent recent study by Michael Mallett, *The Borgias: The Rise and Fall of a Renaissance Dynasty* (London: Paladin, 1971).

26. *History of Italy*, pp. 319, 321.

27. Ibid., p. 231.

28. Ibid., p. 182.

29. Ibid., p. 331.

30. Gilbert, *Machiavelli and Guicciardini*, pp. 251 - 52, 292 - 93, discusses Vettori and Guicciardini and their respective judgments on *fortuna* and the two Medici popes.

31. *History of Italy*, p. 362.

32. Ibid., p. 363.

33. Ibid., p. 57.

34. *Machiavelli and Guicciardini*, p. 269.

35. *The Prince and the Discourses*, p. 91.

36. Ibid., p. 94.

37. *History of Italy*, p. 3.

38. John R. Hale, "Introduction" to Guicciardini, *History of Italy and History of Florence*, p. xxi.

39. *History of Italy*, p. 155.

40. Ibid., pp. 101 - 2.

41. Ibid., p. 276.

42. Ibid., p. 63.

43. Ibid., p. 385.

44. Ibid., p. 398.

45. *Machiavelli and Guicciardini*, p. 300.

Chapter Nine

1. For the information on the various translations of Guicciardini's works, the indispensable study by Vincenzo Luciani, *Francesco Guicciardini e la fortuna dell'opera sua*, is the most complete and authoritative analysis

available. Other works of interest are Rudolf B. Gottfried, *Geoffrey Fenton's Historie of Guicciardini*, Indiana Univ. Humanities Series, No. 3 (Bloomington, 1940); Paolo Guicciardini, *La storia guicciardiniana nelle traduzioni francesi* (Florence, 1950); and *La storia guicciardiniana nelle traduzioni inglesi* (Florence, 1951), also by Paolo Guicciardini.

2. *Plusieurs Advis et Conseils de François Guicciardin, tant pour les affaires d'Estat que privées, traduits d'Italien en François par A. de Laval avec quarante et deux articles concernants ce mesme subject* (Paris, 1576); cited in Luciani, ibid., p. 473.

3. Luciani, ibid., p. 322.

4. Ibid., p. 473.

5. Ibid., p. 323.

6. *The Maxims of Francesco Guicciardini* (London, 1845).

7. Luciani, *Francesco Guicciardini e la fortuna dell'opera sua*, pp. 324 - 27, discusses this and other such collections.

8. I refer to the previously cited editions by Cecil Grayson (*Selected Writings*) and Mario Domandi (*Maxims and Reflections*).

9. Luciani, *Francesco Guicciardini e la fortuna dell'opera sua*, p. 32.

10. Ibid., p. 132.

11. Here, Paolo Guicciardini, *La storia guicciardiniana nelle traduzioni francesi*, p. 11., disagrees with Luciani's dating of the first French edition. He maintains that the translation was done in 1566 but was printed with a publication date of 1568; Luciani accepts 1568 as the correct date without noting any earlier date of composition.

12. See Paolo Guicciardini, ibid., pp. 11 - 27, for a discussion of this translation, its importance, and its various editions.

13. *Francisci Guicciardini Loci duo, ob rerum quas continent gravitatem cognitione dignissimi, qui ex ipsius historiarum libris III et IV dolo malo detracti, in exemplaribus hactenus impressis non leguntur* (cited by Luciani, *Francesco Guicciardini*, p. 209). The work is usually known as the *Loci duo*.

14. For a more detailed study of Fenton and his translation, see Gottfried, *Geoffrey Fenton's Historie*, or Paolo Guicciardini's *La storia guicciardiniana nelle traduzioni inglesi*, or Luciani, ibid., p. 35.

15. *The History of Italy, from the Year 1490, to 1532. Written in Italian by Francesco Guicciardini, etc. In Twenty Books. Translated into English by the Chevalier Austin Parke Goddard* (London, 1753 - 1756), cited by Luciani, ibid., p. 50.

16. For information on the Spanish versions and a comparison of them with the Italian original, see Luciani, ibid., pp. 36 - 37.

17. For particulars on this historical curiosity, see ibid., p. 398.

18. *Method for the Easy Comprehension of History*, trans. Beatrice Reynolds (New York: Columbia University Press, 1945), pp. 61, 73.

19. Ibid., pp. 73 - 74.

20. *The Complete Essays of Montaigne*, trans. Donald Frame (Stanford: Stanford University Press, 1958), p. 305.

21. Ibid.

22. Ibid.

23. Luciani, *Francesco Guicciardini e la fortuna dell' opera sua*, p.300 - 1.

24. Ibid., p. 253.

25. For an extensive consideration of this relationship, see ibid., pp. 301 - 2; or Vincenzo Luciani, "Bacon and Guicciardini," *PMLA* 62 (1947), 96 - 113.

26. "Bacon and Guicciardini," p. 112.

27. For a study of Guicciardini and his formulation of the concept of the balance of power, see Ernest W. Nelson, "The Origins of Modern Balance-of-Power Politics," *Medievalia et Humanistica* 1 (1943), 124 - 42. Guicciardini may have glimpsed a hint of this concept from his reading of the unpublished *De Bello italico commentarius* by Bernardo Rucellai (1449 - 1514), which he read in manuscript form.

28. Cited from "Of Empire" in *The Essays or Counsels, Civill and Morall* in *Francis Bacon: A Selection of His Works*, ed. Sidney Warhaft (New York: Odyssey Press, 1965), pp. 94 - 95.

29. Luciani, *Francesco Guicciardini e la fortuna dell'opera sua*, p. 303.

30. Gottfried, *Geoffrey Fenton's Historie of Guicciardin*, p. 5.

31. Luciani, *Francesco Guicciardini e la fortuna dell'opera sua*, p. 33.

32. Ibid., pp. 182 - 83, 431.

33. P. Sarpi, *The Historie of the Councel of Trent etc. Faithfully translated into English by N. Brent. Unto this Second Edition are added divers observable Passages, and Epistles concerning the trueth of this Historie* etc. London, 1629; cited by Luciani in ibid., p. 211.

34. Gilbert Highet, *The Classical Tradition: Greek and Roman Influences on Western Literature* (New York: Oxford University Press, 1967), pp. 261 - 92, contains an excellent summary of this literary phenomenon.

35. Cited by Luciani, *Francesco Guicciardini e la fortuna dell'opera sua,* p. 294.

36. Jonathan Swift, *Gulliver's Travels and Other Writings*, ed. Louis A. Landa (New York: Houghton Mifflin, 1960), p. 369.

37. Henry St. John, Lord Viscount Bolingbroke, *Letters on the Study and Use of History* (London: Murray, 1870), p. 41.

38. *The English Essays of Edward Gibbon*, ed. Patricia B. Craddock (Oxford: Clarendon Press, 1972), pp. 94 - 95.

39. *Oeuvres de Voltaire*, ed. M. Beuchot (Paris: Lefèvre, 1829), XVII, 182 (my translation).

40. Ibid., pp. 83 - 84, 91, 94 - 95.

41. *History of Italian Literature*, II, 593.

42. Ibid., II, 590.

43. *Saggi critici*, p. 23 (my translation).

44. Ibid., p. 25 (my translation).

45. "Introduction," Francesco Guicciardini, *History of Italy and History of Florence*, p. vii.

46. Jacob Burckhardt, *The Civilization of the Renaissance in Italy*, ed. Irene Gordon (New York: Mentor, 1961), p. 86.

Selected Bibliography

PRIMARY SOURCES

1. Italian Editions

Carteggi di Francesco Guicciardini. Edited by Roberto Palmarocchi and Pier Giorgio Ricci. 17 volumes to date. Naples: Istituto Storico Italiano, 1938-.

Le cose fiorentine ora per la prima volta pubblicate. Edited by Roberto Ridolfi. Florence: Olschki, 1945.

Dialogo e discorsi del Reggimento di Firenze. Edited by Roberto Palmarocchi. Bari: Laterza, 1932.

Opere. Edited by Emanuella Lugnani Scarano. Turin: UTET, 1970.

Opere. Edited by Vittorio De Caprariis. Milan: Mondadori, 1953.

Opere inedite. Edited by Giuseppe Canestrini. 10 vols. Florence: Barbèra, 1857 - 67.

Ricordi. Edited by Roberto Palmarocchi. Bari: Laterza, 1933.

Ricordi: edizione critica. Edited by Raffaello Spongano. Florence: Sansoni, 1951.

Scritti autobiografici e rari. Edited by Roberto Palmarocchi. Bari: Laterza, 1936.

Scritti politici e ricordi. Edited by Roberto Palmarocchi. Bari: Laterza, 1933.

Storie fiorentine. Edited by Roberto Palmarocchi. Bari: Laterza, 1931.

Storia d'Italia. Edited by Silvana Seidel Menchi. Introduction by Felix Gilbert. 3 vols. Turin: Einaudi, 1971.

Storia d'Italia. Edited by Constantino Panigada. 5 vols. Bari: Laterza, 1929.

2. English Translations

The History of Florence. Translated by Mario Domandi. New York: Harper & Row, 1970. An outstanding translation of the complete history including a superb introduction and a very useful glossary of Florentine political terms.

The History of Italy. Translated by Sidney Alexander. New York: Macmillan, 1969 (paperback edition, New York: Collier, 1973). An excellent translation profusely illustrated by maps and prints of the period,

153

containing ample historical notes. Sections omitted by the translator
are paraphrased for the reader's convenience.

The History of Italy and History of Florence. Translated by Cecil Grayson.
Introduction by John H. Hale. New York: Twayne, 1964. Well translated and edited, this edition provides generous and convenient selections from both major historical works by Guicciardini in one volume.

Maxims and Reflections (Ricordi). Translated by Mario Domandi. Introduction by Nicolai Rubinstein. Philadelphia: University of Penn-
sylvania Press, 1972. The best English edition of the *Ricordi* by virtue
of its inclusion of not only Manuscript C but also B, Q^1, and Q^2.
Rubinstein's preface is enlightening, and the table comparing the versions of the individual maxims is very useful.

Selected Writings. Edited and with an introduction by Cecil Grayson.
Translated by Margaret Grayson. London: Oxford University Press,
1965. A good translation of the final version of the *Ricordi* plus the
only available English translations of both the *Ricordanze* and the
Considerations on the 'Discourses' of Machiavelli.

SECONDARY SOURCES

BENOIST, EUGENE. *Guichardin historien et homme d'état florentin au XVI*e
siècle. Paris-Marseilles: Librairie Générale, 1862. One of the first
studies of Guicciardini's life and works, marred by prejudice and
proved faulty by recent discoveries.

BONDANELLA, PETER E. *Machiavelli and the Art of Renaissance History.*
Detroit: Wayne State University Press, 1973. In addition to a consideration of the Guicciardini-Machiavelli friendship and correspondence, this study deals with many of the stylistic features of
Renaissance prose which have a bearing on Guicciardini's style as well
as key Machiavellian concepts which Guicciardini rejects or accepts
only in part.

DE CAPRARIIS, VITTORIO. *Francesco Guicciardini: dalla politica alla storia.*
Bari: Laterza, 1950. Lucid analysis of Guicciardini's progress from the
early ideologically oriented works to those more objective and
historical in nature.

DE SANCTIS, FRANCESCO. *The History of Italian Literature.* 2 vols. Translated by Joan Redfern. New York: Basic Books, 1959; Reprint of a
1931 edition. The chapter on Machiavelli contains a very influential
comparison of Guicciardini and Machiavelli.

———. *Saggi Critici.* Edited by Luigi Russo. 3 vols. Bari: Laterza, 1971.
The important essay entitled "L'uomo del Guicciardini" reflects the
Risorgimento's distaste for Guicciardini's personality, but the study
still merits reading and debate.

GAGNEUX, MARCEL. "Idéologie et opportunisme chez François Guichardin: l'homme du 'oui mais'." In *Les Écrivains et le pouvoir en Italie à l'époque de la renaissance.* Edited by André Rochon. Paris: Universitaire de la Sorbonne Nouvelle, 1973. A lengthy, detailed account of the relationship between Guicciardini's theory and his actual political practice.

————. "Nature et condition humaines selon François Guichardin." *Revue des Études Italiennes* 16 (1970), 231 - 63. A summary of Guicciardini's views on human nature in his collected works.

GILBERT, FELIX. *Machiavelli and Guicciardini: Politics and History in Sixteenth-Century Florence.* Princeton: Princeton University Press, 1965. An excellent study of humanist historiography and of the relationship between political events and the composition of history and political theory during this period in Florence.

GOLDTHWAITE, RICHARD A. *Private Wealth in Renaissance Florence: A Study of Four Families.* Princeton: Princeton University Press, 1968. A presentation of a wealth of archival material on the backgrounds of major Florentine families, including the Guicciardini, set within a general discussion of the place of the families and their fortunes in Renaissance Florence.

GOTTFRIED, RUDOLF B. *Geoffrey Fenton's Historie of Guicciardin.* Indiana University Humanities Series, No. 3. Bloomington: Indiana University Press, 1940. A brief analysis of Fenton's sixteenth-century English translation, useful for the light it sheds upon English views of Italy during the period.

GUICCIARDINI, PAOLO. *Le traduzioni francesi della storia guicciardiniana.* Florence: Olschki, 1950. A scholarly survey of French versions of *The History of Italy.*

————. *Le traduzioni inglesi della storia guicciardiniana.* Florence: Olschki, 1951. A companion volume to the above study, analyzing English versions of *The History of Italy.*

————, and DORI, EMILIO. *Le antiche case ed il palazzo dei Guicciardini in Firenze.* Florence: Olschki, 1952. A discussion of the history of the family palace in Florence with good illustrations of its archives and library.

LUCIANI, VINCENZO. "Bacon and Guicciardini." *PMLA* 62 (1947), 96 - 113. A study of Bacon's knowledge and use of Guicciardini's works.

————. *Francesco Guicciardini e la fortuna dell'opera sua.* Florence: Olschki, 1949; originally published as *Francesco Guicciardini and his European Reputation* (New York: K. Otto, 1936). A monumental over-view of Guicciardini's reception abroad and within Italy, indispensable to any consideration of the problem.

————. "Il Guicciardini e la Spagna." *PMLA* 56 (1941), 992 - 1006. A good treatment of Guicciardini's years as ambassador in Spain and of the writings that resulted from them.

MALAGODI, LUIGI. *Guicciardini*. Florence: La Nuova Italia, 1939. A somewhat shallow biographical study of Guicciardini and his works, now outdated.

OTETEA, ANDRÉ. *François Guichardin: sa vie publique et sa pensée politique*. Paris: Picart, 1926. Although now rendered somewhat obsolete by subsequent discoveries, this is an adequate account of Guicciardini's life and thought.

POCOCK, J. G. A. *The Machiavellian Moment: Florentine Political Thought and the Atlantic Republican Tradition*. Princeton: Princeton University Press, 1975. Contains the most detailed analyses of Guicciardini's minor political treatises available, setting them within the context of republican theory in sixteenth-century Italy.

RAMAT, RAFFAELLO. *Il Guicciardini e la tragedia d'Italia*. Florence: Olschki, 1953. One of the best critical works on Guicciardini available in Italian. Ramat's ideas are widely accepted by most critics, especially his view of *The History of Italy* as a tragedy.

RIDOLFI, ROBERTO. *La genesi della Storia d'Italia guicciardiniana*. Florence: Olschki, 1939. A seminal work which opened the way for all contemporary studies of Guicciardini's methods in the composition of *The History of Italy*.

————. *The Life of Francesco Guicciardini*. Translated by Cecil Grayson. New York: Knopf, 1968; original Italian edition, Rome: Belardetti, 1960. A masterful critical biography, the single most important study of Guicciardini in any language.

————. *The Life of Niccolò Machiavelli*. Translated by Cecil Grayson. Chicago: University of Chicago Press, 1963; original Italian edition, Rome: Belardetti; 1954. Ridolfi's greatest biography, an excellent source for information concerning the friendship and correspondence between Machiavelli and Guicciardini.

RUBINSTEIN, NICOLAI. "The *Storie fiorentine* and the *Memorie di famiglia* by Francesco Guicciardini." *Rinascimento* 4 (1953), 171 - 225. A very useful analysis of the links between family diaries and Guicciardini's first writings.

SCARANO, EMANUELLA LUGNANI. "Il dialogo *Del Reggimento di Firenze* di Francesco Guicciardini." *Giornale storico della letteratura italiana* 145 (1968), 232 - 92, 523 - 60. An extremely important study of Guicciardini's early political dialogue which shows how the work is related to the future development of Guicciardini's political ideas.

————. *Guicciardini e la crisi del Rinascimento*. Bari: Laterza, 1973. Part of a critical history of Italian literature in the "Letteratura italiana Laterza" series, this work contains ample texts and critical or historical commentaries and is an excellent introduction to Guicciardini's life and works.

————. "Le redazioni dei *Ricordi* e la storia del pensiero guicciardiniano dal 1512 al 1530." *Giornale storico della letteratura italiana* 147 (1970),

181 - 259. A very informative analysis of the various stylistic and philosophical changes in different versions of the *Ricordi* and their significance in the evolution of Guicciardini's thought.

SPIRITO, UGO. *Machiavelli e Guicciardini*. Florence: Sansoni, 1945. A general overview of the major ideas of these two political writers and a comparison of their works.

STARN, RANDOLPH. "Francesco Guicciardini and his Brothers." In *Renaissance Studies in Honor of Hans Baron*. Edited by Anthony Molho and John A. Tedeschi. Dekalb: Northern Illinois University Press, 1971. A valuable supplement to Goldthwaite's work on the Guicciardini family.

VITALE, VITO. *Francesco Guicciardini*. Turin: UTET, 1941. A general treatment of Guicciardini's life and times combined with brief analyses of his major works which is less useful than the Ridolfi biography and now somewhat outdated.

VON ALBERTINI, RUDOLF. *Firenze dalla repubblica al principato: storia e coscienza politica*. Turin: Einaudi, 1970; original German edition published in 1955. An important treatment of political events and historical or political works, including those of Guicciardini, during the same period as that analyzed by Felix Gilbert.

Index

(The works of Guicciardini are listed under his name)

158

DATE DUE

GAYLORD			PRINTED IN U.S.A.